T

WOLF B.

WITH APPRECIATION
FOR YOUR EXCELLENCE
IN REPORTING AND
WITH ASPIRATIONS
FOR MORE TOLERANCE
AND LESS HATRED
IN OUR WORLD,

Richard G. (Dick) Dumont
APRIL, 2013

Copyright © 2013 by Richard G. Dumont
First Edition – February 2013

ISBN
978-1-4602-1236-3 (Hardcover)
978-1-4602-1237-0 (Paperback)
978-1-4602-1238-7 (eBook)

Produced by:

FriesenPress

Suite 300 – 852 Fort Street
Victoria, BC, Canada V8W 1H8

www.friesenpress.com

Distributed to the trade by The Ingram Book Company

WHEN HATE HAPPENS, SO DOES OTHER BAD STUFF:

Respect Diversity – Teach Tolerance – Fight Hate!

Richard G. Dumont, Ph.D.

Advance Praise For This Book

When Hate Happens ... is a passionate and exhaustively researched treatise on hate that covers the psychological, physiological, and sociological elements of the darker side of human nature. The balance of qualitative (emotional appeal) and quantitative arguments (the hate rate) is delicate and effective. The friendly style of writing that readers saw in 'Economic Inequality...', combined with a clear mastery of the subject matter, make the book informative, compelling, and easy to digest.

The wrtiting style and quality are excellent throughout the book, and the content is exceptionally well structured, referenced, and argued ... The timely advice and thorough examination of the topic will make it an important book for anyone to read, either American or not, as we collectively try to grapple with an increasingly polarized world.

Eric Anderson

Dedicated

to
Elizabeth, Katherine,
Peter and Ashley
for your living
exemplary lives embracing
love, tolerance, and truth
from
your appreciative and proud
Dad

They're rioting in Africa
They're starving in Spain
There's hurricanes in Florida
And Texas needs rain
The whole world is festering
With unhappy souls
The French hate the Germans
The Germans hate the Poles
Italians hate Yugoslavs
South Africans hate the Dutch
And I don't like anybody very much
But we can be tranquil
And thankful and proud
For man's been endowed
With a mushroom shaped cloud
And we know for certain
That some lovely day
Someone will set the spark off
And we will all be blown away!
They're rioting in Africa
There's strife in Iran
What nature doesn't do to us
Will be done by our fellow man

Lyrics to the song,
"Merry Little Minuet"
The Kingston Trio, 1959

This cavern is below all, and the enemy of all;
it is hatred, without exception.

Victor Hugo
Les Misérables

Darkness cannot drive out darkness: only light can do that.
Hate cannot drive out hate: only love can do that ...
Hatred paralyzes life; love releases it.
Hatred confuses life; love harmonizes it.
Hatred darkens life; love illuminates it ...
I have decided to stick to love...
Hate is too great a burden to bear ....

Dr. Martin Luther King Jr.,
A Testament of Hope
The Essential Writings
and Speeches

Animals don't hate, and we're supposed to be better than them.

Elvis Presley

Hate is an automatic response to fear, for fear humiliates.

Graham Greene,
The Human Factor

Hate is the father of all evil.

David Gemmell,
Fall of Kings

Table of Contents

Acknowledgements

This book, like my most recent, *Economic Inequality and What YOU Can Do About It: A Primer and Call to Action!*, would not have been possible without the assistance of my extraordinarily intelligent and precious wife, Nancy, who is my dedicated and experienced first-reader, demandingly meticulous and exacting copy editor, and indefatigable cheerleader. What a winning combination. I'm a lucky guy.

I have benefited greatly from her infinite patience, encouragement, editorial assistance, and substantive contributions, as I have also from the feedback provided by my dear and supportive friends Joyce Bates, Mike Bogolea, John Dalphin, and Joan Howard.

This book would never have materialized were it not for the enduring and exceptionally fine work of the co-founders, chief legal counsel, and president at the Southern Poverty Law Center (SPLC), including their very capable associates and staff.

SPLC Senior Fellow, Mark Potok, in particular, has been especially cooperative and helpful to me by answering my numerous questions regarding the processes and procedures used by the SPLC in identifying, classifying, recording, and enumerating active hate groups on a state-by-state basis in the United States. I am forever grateful to him and happily remain in his debt.

I have the utmost respect for the SPLC, its mission, and its exemplary work in pursuing goals and objectives foundational to and consistent with those articulated in the subtitle of this book, *Respect Diversity – Teach Tolerance – Fight Hate!*

I am very much indebted to William G. Miller, Emeritus Professor at Iowa State University, whose versatile and comprehensive *Open Stat* statistical package has allowed me to analyze the data of the current study as well as those of my several other research efforts of recent years. Bill has also been most kind and patient in promptly responding to my several email queries regarding detailed technical matters.

Susan Mayo of FriesenPress has been indispensably helpful in assisting me complete the various practical chores involved in the production of this book.

Any and all errors in this manuscript are mine.

Preface

Why would anybody want to write a book about hate? That's a good question, especially since, as you shall discover in the pages that follow, hate is one of those defining characteristics of humankind by which we are actually dehumanized.

Hate brings out the very worst of which we are capable: the vile, the disgusting, and the contemptible.

Hate corrupts us, diminishes us, and it is destructive, both of the haters themselves, and of the targets of their hate.

As the scruffy looking banditos appearing in the Sergio Leone Spaghetti Western, *A Fistful of Dollars*, starring Clint Eastwood, might have said, "Hate? Hate? We don't need no stinkin' hate."

Similarly, as the title of the popular John Lennon and Paul McCartney Beatles song, also aptly says, "All We Need Is Love."

If I had written this book about love, I could have used the Beatles' song in my epigraph rather than the one by The Kingston Trio, even though I find the lyrics to the "Merry Little Minuet" to be much more creative and, actually, quite funny.

Speaking of funny, and despite the seriousness of the subject of hate, you will find that I attempt to interject a little humor throughout the book. I do this, not because I find anything at all funny about manifest hate, but, rather because I have learned through my many years of living that humor is a very important and necessary part of life.

Humor helps us to cope with those otherwise totally discouraging and depressing realities that we discover daily about the human condition.

Humor is also cathartic, and it has even been used deliberately in certain forms of emotional-healing therapy.

As Annette Goodheart has written in her 1994 book, *Laughter Therapy: How to Laugh About Everything in Your Life That Isn't Really Funny*, for example:

> Cathartic psychotherapy emphasizes and utilizes laughter as one of the major cathartic processes healing emotional pain. It is specific to the release of light anger, light fear, and boredom. When people laugh, if uncomplicated by medications which may interfere with the physical catharsis, they are releasing painful feeling which is gone for all time ...What we don't realize is that when we lose control of our feelings cathartically, we actually gain 'control of our lives in flexible, intelligent, creative, and caring ways.' (1994, p. 36).

Now, I don't expect you to laugh at, snicker about, or even appreciate all or most of my attempts at humor. In fact, as you encounter my attempts at humor hither and yon, the latter location and locution might be better expressed when spelled as 'yawn.'

Writing humor can be difficult and it is almost always risky; you risk annoying, turning off, or even offending the reader.

Even, my wife, Nancy, who loves me very much, occasionally moans at my "groaners."

Hey, nobody's perfect.

Well, let's get back to the Beatles and their "Love, love, love. Love is all we need."

Love may very well be all we need, but we also have, like it or not, hate.

I would certainly rather be writing a book about love. For one thing, I know much more, at the personal level, about love than I do about hate. I am a 72 year old happy and well-seasoned retiree, who for most of my life, has been surrounded by love and loved ones, including my wife, Nancy, and our children, Elizabeth, Katherine, Peter, and Ashley, who also know about and continue to live lives affirming love.

I chose to write a book about hate because, as a human being and as a sociologist, I perceive manifest hate to be a serious social problem or indicator of societal dysfunction.

I feel a moral and professional obligation to share my knowledge in hopes that we can work together to reduce hate and its associated bad accoutrements.

Hate is a subject that I have been researching, as a social scientist, since 2007, the year I first became acquainted with the work of the Southern Poverty Law Center (SPLC). The SPLC's very *raison d'etre* is to encourage and assist all of us to respect diversity, teach tolerance, and fight hate.

So inspired was I by the work of the SPLC, that I actually utilized their compiled and published numbers on active hate groups in the 50 U.S. States and Washington, D.C., to develop my own data base that has allowed me to conduct my unique sociological research on hate. You will find the results of my research reported and discussed in Chapter 5.

I hope that by reading this book you will come better to understand the biological, emotional, psychological, and sociological bases, dynamics, and manifestations of hate.

Furthermore, and most importantly, I anticipate that your increased knowledge will prepare and motivate you to take action to fight hate and to increase tolerance and respect for diversity at every opportunity that presents itself. Some suggestions about where you might begin appear in my Chapter 6.

As in my recent book, *Economic Inequality and What YOU Can Do About It: A Primer and Call to Action!*, I have tried to communicate with you primarily by relying upon our shared common sense and also upon down-to-earth sociology.

You are the final judge as to whether or not I succeed in persuasively making my case in common sense and down-to-earth sociology terms that are comprehensible to and that resonate with you.

After you have finished reading the book, and actually anytime at all while you are in the process of reading it, I would be most happy to receive your reactions to it, as well as to answer any questions that you might have.

Just send me a message at my email address, and I promise to get back to you.

Richard G. Dumont, Ph.D.
Greenville, South Carolina
September 5, 2012
Email address: whenhatehappens@gmail.com

PART I

When Hate Happens

Introduction

The killing rampages of Timothy McVeigh, Jared Lee Loughner, Anders Behring Breivik, and Wade Michael Page, whether inspired by extremist ideologies and/or triggered by brief or lasting periods of insanity, were raw demonstrations of unbridled and deadly *manifest hate*.

On April 19, 1995, "Oklahoma City Bomber" Tim McVeigh detonated a truck bomb in front of the Alfred P. Murrah Building, killing 168 and injuring over 800.

According to the Southern Poverty Law Center (SPLC), which monitors anti-government militia and patriot groups, "Timothy McVeigh, the Oklahoma City bomber, was motivated by extreme anti-government beliefs then circulating in the militia movement. He was also inspired by the racist novel, *The Turner Diaries*, modeling his attack on a scene from the book."

On January 8, 2011, 22 year old Jared Lee Loughner, armed with a semi-automatic Glock pistol equipped with a 30-round clip of 9 mm bullets, unleashed a barrage of shots in front of a Safeway grocery store in Tuscan, Arizona, where U.S. Representative Gabrielle Giffords was hosting an open meeting with her constituents and supporters.

The representative was critically injured and 6 persons died at the scene, including U.S. District Judge John Roll, Giffords staff member, Gabriel Zimmerman, and 9 year old Christina Taylor Green. Several others at the site were wounded, with a total of 19 persons shot before Loughner could load another 30-round clip into his deadly weapon; he was subdued before inflicting more carnage.

While mental illness appeared the most likely explanation for his behavior, mainstream media coverage of the shootings also presented some evidence suggesting Loughner's hatred of women, government, and all religion, especially Christianity. Representative Giffords is a Jew.

On July 21, 2011, Norwegian terrorist Anders Behring Breivik bombed several buildings in Oslo, killing 8, and then went on a shooting rampage at a camp of the Workers' Youth League (AUF) where he ended the lives of 69 others, mostly teenagers.

In the fall, 2011, issue of the Southern Poverty Law Center's *Intelligence Report*, Breivik was described as a "Christian Crusader" who "saw himself as a Christian warrior in the midst of what he called an 'existential conflict' with Islam – a modern knight confronting hordes at the gates of the West. His 1,500-page manifesto, titled '2083: A European Declaration of Independence' and released just hours before the July 22 massacre, is a call to arms against 'cultural Marxism' – a term describing the white nationalist notion that multiculturalists are working to destroy Western civilization."

On August 5, 2012, 40 year old Wade Michael Page, carrying a 9-millimeter semi-automatic handgun and displaying a 9/11 tattoo on his left shoulder, killed 5 men and 1 woman at the Sikh Temple in Oak Creek, Wisconsin, the victims ranging in age from 39 to 84.

The Southern Poverty Law Center (SPLC), which monitors hate groups, "had been tracking him for years and described him as a Neo-Nazi. Mr. Page was well known in the white power subculture, posting hundreds of messages on supremacist Web sites and playing in bands called Definite Hate and End Apathy."

I don't know about you, but in each and every of the above instances, when I first learned the surprising news about these horrific murders, my reactions were shock, incredulity, outrage, sadness, and disappointment.

I was shocked that such massacres could occur in these supposedly modern and civilized times, incredulous that they could actually happen, angered to the point of outrage at the perpetrators of those heinous crimes, saddened at the loss of life of the victims and the grief of their surviving family and friends, and disappointed that members of our species could be so motivated by cruelty and hatred toward others, based on group affiliations, such as gender, race, and religion, as to be driven to these inexcusable and unspeakable acts of callous inhumanity.

Now, all of us are capable of hatred and most of us do hate from time-to-time. Former U.S. President George H.W. Bush hated broccoli and President William (Bill) Jefferson Clinton hated having to give up hamburgers, French fries, and milk shakes.

According to my tried, trusted, and well-worn, like me, *Merriam Webster's Collegiate Dictionary*, the noun, 'hate' is defined thusly:

1. a. intense hostility and aversion usually deriving from fear, anger, or sense of injury
   b. extreme dislike or antipathy: LOATHING (had a great loathing of hard work)

2. an object of hatred (a generation whose finest hate had been big business).

   The definition of 'hate' as a verb is:

3. to feel extreme enmity toward (hates his country's enemies)

4. to have a strong aversion to: find very distasteful (hated to have to meet strangers); (hated hypocrisy) : to express or feel extreme enmity or active hostility; (hates one's guts) ; to hate someone with great intensity.

As you can see from the above definitions, we use both the noun and the verb 'hate' in many different ways and in equally numerous and different contexts.

We've all said "I hate" something or someone, but what did we really mean? Were we angry, jealous, or just annoyed? Did we dislike the way something tasted? For a teenager confronting his or her parents, "I hate you" might actually mean "I hate your rules."

In some cases our associated feelings are emotional and intense, while in others they are less so.

There is a difference, of course, between saying that you hate a person, or food, or bad drivers who cut in front of you without signaling, and feeling such rage that you are prone to become violent and/or commit a violent act.

Many of us hate snakes, spiders, poison mushrooms, castor oil, liver and onions, cold pizza, the salmonella virus, laziness, over-ambition, gluttony, dirty laundry, unmade beds, unshaven faces or legs, cigarette smoke, smelly rotted potatoes or dirty socks, un-cut lawns, un-manicured shrubs and fingernails, rainy days, cold winters, high humidity, being overcharged at the cash register, spilling red wine on a white carpet, things that go bump in the night, taxes, and the thought of death, especially our own.

Having these kinds of hatreds is normal, part of what it means to be human, and they are common features of everyday life.

These are not the kinds of hate that are my concern in this book.

My focus, rather, is on those hatreds that are directed against a group or category of people, because of their perceived, real or imagined, differences; namely, differences based on ethnicity, race, religion, age, gender, sexual orientation, political affiliation, and positions on a wide variety of economic, political, and social issues, such as abortion, free-speech, economic equality, fairness, and so on.

It is precisely these kinds of *in-group* versus *out-group* hatreds that appeared as prominent motivations in the killing rampages of previously mentioned murderers Timothy McVeigh, Jared Lee Loughner, Anders Behring Breivik, and (allegedly, at the time of this writing) Wade Michael Page.

This book, *When Hate Happens, So Does Other Bad Stuff: Respect Diversity – Teach Tolerance – Fight Hate!*, has been written to appeal to a broad, intelligent, thoughtful, and open-minded readership, hopefully representing a broad spectrum of views on political, economic, and social issues.

Whether the reader self-identifies as a liberal/progressive, moderate, or conservative, or as a Democrat, Republican, or Independent, we all have a vested interest in understanding and combating manifest hate.

In writing this book, I have attempted to avoid, in so far as possible, unnecessary and potentially confusing professional psychological and sociological jargon, and I try my very best to communicate with you primarily by relying on common sense and down-to-earth sociology.

I have also tried to simplify and explain in common sense and down-to-earth sociology terms the presentation and interpretation of numbers and statistics that appear in Chapter 5, *Findings from my Own Research on Manifest Hate as Measured by my HATE RATE*, so that a lack of mathematical and statistical sophistication should not be an obstacle to understanding.

If reading my book helps to encourage, energize, mobilize, and give direction to those among us who are tolerant of group and individual differences and impatient with bigots and those who would discriminate against others because of the color of their skin, where and how they worship, their gender, and sexual preferences, while simultaneously broadening the perspectives of those who are less tolerant and less accepting of group differences, if only even a little bit, then I will have been at least somewhat successful.

As for the hapless haters among us, who hopefully are a reasonably small minority of Americans, I have minimal expectations of penetrating their well-armored shells of smug, self-satisfied ignorance and inexcusable self-centeredness, and any and all attempts on my part to change their minds are probably a waste of my precious time.

I hope that by reading my work you will come to agree with me that manifest hate, along with economic inequality, which was the topic of my previous book, *Economic Inequality and What YOU Can Do About It: A Primer and Call to Action!*, is one of the most immediate and important social issues of our time, and that what we choose to do or not to do about it will ultimately determine the character and very fate of our ever-so-fragile democracy.

In the pages that follow, I will attempt to summarize what psychologists and sociologists have learned about the subject of hate; present evidence from my own sociological research that demonstrates that manifest hate relates in many predictable and depressing ways to a wide variety of social problems or measures of societal dysfunction; and suggest ways that you and I might become actively involved in promoting respect for diversity, teaching tolerance, and fighting hate.

In writing this book, I have been committed, not only to attempting to communicate with you in terms of both common sense and down-to-earth sociology, but also by being totally honest and up-front from beginning to end.

In that regard, I feel obliged to forewarn you that Chapters 1 through 5, which present and discuss the findings of early research on hate, the psychology of hate, the duplex theory of hate, the sociology of hate, and the findings of my own sociological research on hate, will require more focused attention on your part as the reader. Such is the reality of reading summaries of the psychological and sociological literature on hate. Please be patient. I will be ever-so-grateful for your being so.

Here we go. Get aboard the Respect Diversity – Teach Tolerance – Fight Hate Express!

CHAPTER 1
Early Research on Hate

In 1950, psychologists Else Frenkel-Brunswick, Daniel Levinson, and Nevitt Sanford teamed up with sociologist Theodor Adorno to write *The Authoritarian Personality*, a ground-breaking work whose principal research findings and generalizations are reflected in numerous subsequent research studies and theories about hate.

For example, recently retired University of Manitoba psychologist Bob Altemeyer spent the better part of his career studying the authoritarian personality and its correlates.

In his 2006 book, *The Authoritarians*, Altemeyer characterized religious fundamentalists as being right-wing "authoritarian followers," who are easily and readily manipulated into ideologies of hate by authoritarian leaders, and:

> They are highly submissive to established authority, aggressive in the name of that authority, and conventional to the point of insisting everyone should behave as their authorities decide. They are fearful and self-righteous and have a lot of hostility in them that they readily direct toward various out groups. They are easily incited, easily led, rather un-inclined to think for themselves, largely impervious to facts and reason, and rely instead on social support to maintain their beliefs. They bring strong loyalty to their in-groups, have

> thick-walled, highly compartmentalized minds, use a lot of double standards in their judgments, are surprisingly unprincipled at times, and are often hypocrites (2006, p.140).

Does this characterization describe a person or persons whom you have read about, heard, or seen interviewed on mainstream media recently, or maybe someone you know, personally?

Sadly, I have known and continue to know quite a few, although I tend to avoid them like I give wide berth to poisonous snakes, whenever possible. Opening and changing their minds is generally a lost cause, for reasons evident in the above quote.

Psychologist Gordon Allport in his widely-cited *The Nature of Prejudice* (1954) developed a psychosociological theory in which prejudice was foundational to the explanation of the development of hate, including hate's several components and manifestations.

Allport defined hate as:

> ... a sentiment – an enduring organization of impulses toward a person or toward a class of persons. Since it is composed of habitual bitter feeling and accusatory thought, it constitutes a stubborn structure in the mental-emotional life of the individual. By its very nature, hatred is extro-punitive, which means that the hater is sure that the fault lies in the object of his hate.

> So long as he believes this he will not feel guilty for his uncharitable state of mind (1954, p. 341).

Furthermore:

> There is a good reason why out-groups are often chosen as the object of hate and aggression rather than individuals. One human being is, after all, pretty much like any other – like oneself. One can scarcely help

but sympathize with the victim. To attack him would be to arouse pain in ourselves. Our own 'body image' would be involved, for his body is like our body. But there is no body image of a group. It is more abstract, more impersonal...

A different colored skin removes the person from our own circle. We are less likely to consider him an individual, and more likely to think of him only as an out-group member (1954, p. 41).

Among the various life experiences contributing to an individual's predisposition to hate, including those of early childhood, Allport singles out *economic insecurity* in adult life:

... downward mobility, periods of unemployment and depression, and general economic dissatisfaction are all positively correlated with prejudice

... The apprehensive and marginal man is vaguely terrified at any signs of ambition or progress on the part of any member of the out-group, whether or not it may constitute a realistic danger (1954, p. 347).

The relationship between economic insecurity and hate is but one of several findings reported in Gordon Allport's theory in *The Nature of Prejudice* that have stimulated and been confirmed by psychologists and sociologists in subsequent research and theories, including my own, as shall be discussed in Chapter 5. It is also confirmed by common sense and down-to-earth sociology.

The reports of a number of research studies by social psychologist Muzafer Sherif, a contemporary of Allport, are also frequently cited as foundational to understanding the manifestations and dynamics of hate, specifically that which develops between groups.

In a number of innovative "natural experiments" designed and conducted by Sherif and his associates, and known as the Robbers Cave

Experiment, begun in Connecticut and concluded in Oklahoma, 1953 through 1961, newly-arrived boys at a summer camp were assigned randomly to two groups that were made to occupy separate living quarters (Sherif, 1988).

In the first stage of the experiment, the groups were allowed to develop their own intra-group interactions and in-group identities whereby they clearly came to see themselves as separate and apart from the out-group.

In subsequent experimental stages, the two groups were made to participate in a series of increasingly competitive zero-sum activities and games, such as baseball and tug-of-war, that increased intra-group solidarity accompanied by inter-group conflict and hostility, manifested in instances of aggression, verbal and even physical.

Incidentally, zero-sum games are those where one side's gains necessarily involve the other side's losses. They are totally and exclusively win or lose situations. In non-zero-sum games, by contrast, both sides may gain through cooperative efforts.

Wouldn't it be great for our country if more Washington, D.C., politicians chose to work together in a non-zero-sum governing framework? Can we really have a functioning 'democracy' when politicians insist on playing their childish tug-of-war, zero-sum, games?

In Sherif's Connecticut experiment, where the groups self-adopted the names of "Red Devils" and "Bull Dogs," a frequently heard chant throughout the camp was "Two, four, six, eight, who do we appreci**hate**!" (emphasis added by me).

In the concluding stages of both the Connecticut and Oklahoma experiments, activities were planned and structured to reduce and resolve inter-group conflict. Specifically, they involved the groups of boys in non-zero-sum games.

The researchers discovered that the most effective conflict resolution strategies were those that set "super-ordinate" goals, that is, goals that could not be attained by either group acting alone, but rather required inter-group cooperation for success.

Whereas the contributions to our understanding of the origins and dynamics of hate by Adorno, et. al., Allport, and Sherif were foundational and substantial, they were actually somewhat tangential to their research and theorizing about the authoritarian personality, prejudice, and behavior within and between small groups, respectively, the phenomenon of hate *per se* has been the explicit focus of a growing body of psychological and sociological research and theorizing.

CHAPTER 2
The Psychology of Hate

B ased upon my own review of the psychology hate-related literature, and I have done a considerable amount, I conclude that hate is best understood as an emotional *and* cognitive, or mental, adaptation rooted in the human evolutionary struggle to survive and reproduce in natural and social environments comprised of numerous threats, including those from animal predators and competing and hostile out-groups.

While societies and cultures undoubtedly play significant and crucial roles in socializing individuals into ideologies of and targets of hate, the roots of hate are, at base, and very importantly, grounded in human emotion.

As evolutionary psychologists John Tooby and Leda Cosmides have so eloquently asserted regarding emotion:

> … an emotion is a superordinate program whose function is to direct the activities and interactions of many subprograms, including those governing perception, attention, inference, learning, memory, goal choice, motivational priorities, categorization and conceptual frameworks, physiological reactions, (e.g., heart rate, endocrine function, immune function, gamete release), reflexes, behavioral decision rules, motor systems, communication processes, energy level and effort allocation, affective coloration of events and stimuli, and the

recalibration of probability estimates, situation assessments, values, and regulatory variables (e.g., self-esteem, estimation of relative formidability, relative value of alternative goal states, efficacy discount rate) (2005, p. 53).

They elaborate further by asserting, again very importantly, that:

An emotion is not reducible to any one category of effects, such as effects on physiology, behavioral inclinations, cognitive appraisals, or feeling states, because it involves evolved instructions for all of them together, as well as other mechanisms distributed throughout the human mental and physical architecture (2005, p.53).

In addition to observing that Tooby and Cosmidies are not committed to easily comprehensible common sense and down-to earth sociology descriptions and explanations, like you and I are, we must agree with their assertion that emotions are, indeed, very important and complicated determinants of human behavior.

To conclude that emotions are somehow less important and relevant than what we like to think about as self-conscious, rational, or purely cognitive thought is to make the very serious mistake of overlooking or denying the points emphasized by their well-substantiated research findings.

Understanding the importance of emotions in activating and sustaining feelings of hate also allows us to appreciate how very difficult it can be to change people's hateful beliefs, attitudes, and behaviors.

You and I have quite a challenge in that regard.

Some researchers have attempted to provide helpful ways of categorizing or organizing emotions.

Primary and Secondary Emotions

One such approach is reflected in attempts to differentiate between the *primary* or lower-order and the *secondary* or higher-order emotions, a strategy that appears consistent with Tooby and Cosmidies recognition of emotions as superordinate programs, which logically allows possibilities for some superordinate programs evolving as superodinate to others, appropriate metaphors being, perhaps, a pyramid or pyramids, or a stack of nesting Russian dolls.

Theodore Kemper, in his "How Many Emotions Are There? Wedding the Social and the Autonomic Components" (1987), identified 4 primary emotions: fear, anger, depression, and satisfaction. Kemper justifies his list of primaries based on "evolutionary, ontogenetic, cross-cultural, physiological, and social relational" evidence (1987, p. 265).

Although Kemper is a sociologist, his work has been influential in bridging the psychology of hate and the sociology of hate, and it also emphasizes the biological bases of the secondary emotion of hate as rooted in the primary emotions of fear and anger.

Kemper argued for the very important role of the *power* and *status* dimensions of social inequality as having particular relevance in eliciting the primary emotions of anger and fear in interactions between and among persons and groups.

Incidentally, the *economic* is a third dimension of social inequality, and it was the subject of my recent book, *Economic Inequality and What YOU Can Do About It: A Primer and Call to Action!*

I encourage you to read it also and also to consider the linkages among the economic, power, and status inequalities and manifest hate.

I have, and they have been the subjects of my ongoing research, some of the results of which you will read about in Chapter 5, *Findings from my Own Research on Manifest Hate as Measured by my HATE RATE.*

Other dimensions of social inequality in the United States include, ethnic, racial, age, gender, and sexual orientation, for example.

Specifically, Kemper hypothesized that, with regard to the power and status dimensions of social inequality:

Fear results from interaction outcomes where actors are subject to the power of others because that power is greater than their own.

Anger results from interaction outcomes in which expected, customary, or deserved status has been denied or withdrawn by another actor who is seen to be responsible for the reduced status.

Depression results from interaction outcomes in which status has been lost or denied, but where the actor deems him - or herself immediately responsible for the loss or incapable of retrieving the desired benefit.

Satisfaction results from interactions in which the power outcome is nonthreatening and the status outcome is according to what was desired and expected.

In this manner, the power and status interaction dimensions link with the primary emotions (1987, p. 275).

It is difficult to overstate the extreme importance of Kemper's argument in assisting our understanding of the dynamics of hate in contemporary America.

When people feel threatened in a period characterized by high levels of unemployment, high levels of income and wealth inequality, high costs for health care, education, housing, food, and for satisfying the other basic needs, elevated levels of both fear and anger are to be expected among larger and larger numbers of citizens.

Such circumstances provide fertile soil for the emergence of hate directed at members of out-groups, who often serve as convenient scapegoats, such as blacks, Muslims, immigrants, pointy-headed liberal intellectuals, and successful women, along with gay, lesbian, bisexual and transgendered persons.

Typically, hate can be directed quite easily at any group or category of persons that members of a particular in-group can conveniently label as the "Other," whether the differences are real or imagined, and whether they are based on skin color, ethnicity, religion, gender, sexual preference, or any number of other social categories that the in-group defines as inferior and unworthy of being accepted as equal.

In Kemper's empirically-based conceptual framework, hate is a *secondary emotion*, which, along with other secondary emotions such as guilt, pride, shame, grief, love, jealousy, and envy, require humans "experiencing one or more of the primaries." Specifically:

> … emotions beyond the primaries are products of social construction through the attachment of social definitions, labels, and meanings to differentiated conditions of interaction and social organization…

> This is a necessary conclusion, since, otherwise, there would be no way to introduce the crucial autonomic component into the secondary emotions; we would be dealing not with emotions but with cognitions only.

> By linking the autonomic arousal of a primary emotion with the process of social construction, we obtain an understanding of secondary emotions that conforms logically and empirically to the known involvement of both the biological and social components (1987, p. 276).

By this statement, Kemper made an additional important contribution to our understanding of the emotional roots and dynamics of hate, and how our biological selves link with our psychological and sociological selves in giving rise to and perpetuating hate.

Biological Foundations of Hate

The basic foundation of our species potential to hate is the human body's autonomic nervous system.

From high school or university biology classes, you may recall that the human body's nervous system is comprised of two major components, the *voluntary* and the *autonomic* systems.

The voluntary one is that which I am primarily relying on right now, at least consciously, as I sit before my computer, alternating my attention between the keypad where I am typing these words and the computer monitor where those words appear, almost as if by magic, before my eyes. My vision and eye movement, except for reflexes, are controlled by my voluntary nervous system.

As you are reading these words, your own voluntary nervous system is doing its work as well.

Lucky us.

That same system allows me to feel the cool air blowing from my ceiling fan and hear the click click from the keyboard as my fingers strike the keys. When I get up for a bathroom break, my voluntary nervous system allows me to control the skeletal muscles that allow me to lift my posterior from the chair and make my legs and arms propel me to my destination, where I hope to find relief. In short, the voluntary nervous system controls bodily skeletal and muscular movement as well as sensation; namely, taste, smell, touch, sight, and hearing.

Unlike the voluntary nervous system, the autonomic one primarily controls functions over which we have less conscious control, including the digestion of food, heart rate, and blood pressure.

The autonomic system itself consists of two branches, the *sympathetic* and the *parasympathetic*.

Very importantly for our present concern with the biological bases of hatred, the sympathetic branch activates the glands and organs against attack.

When threatened by actual or imminent danger, real or imagined, our sympathetic nervous system branch automatically activates our *fight-or-flight*, evolutionary-grounded, readiness to respond to the situation.

More blood is directed by the nerves to the brain and the muscles. Both the heart rate and blood pressure increase. Blood flow to the digestive and waste elimination organs decreases.

Another very important fact to remember about the sympathetic branch of the autonomic nervous system is its *catabolic* function; namely, it operates to tear down or destroy the body.

Our energy is used to prepare for defense, rather than for nourishment or for elimination of wastes.

As Dr. Lawrence Wilson has written, and whose online website contains an informative description of the autonomic nervous system, "An excellent analogy [of the catabolic or defensive nature of the sympathetic branch] is to imagine placing all of the nation's resources in its military defense. While helpful in an emergency, if continued too long, the nation becomes much poorer for lack of productive commercial activity."

The parasympathetic branch of the autonomic nervous system functions to nourish, heal, and regenerate the body.

It is, therefore, very much the opposite of the sympathetic branch. It is *anabolic*, that is, it is concerned with rebuilding the body. Its nerves operate to stimulate digestion, and the waste elimination and immune organs of the body. Among the organs affected are the liver, pancreas, stomach, and intestines.

"The parasympathetic nervous system, when activated by rest, relaxation and happy thoughts, is essential for balanced living and for all healing," to quote Dr. Lawrence once again.

Furthermore, "The sympathetic and parasympathetic systems are antagonistic. Either one or the other is activated most all of the time. The sympathetic system, however, always takes precedence, because it is concerned with one's survival."

"To promote balance and healing, the goal is to keep the sympathetic system turned off as much as possible. This allows the maximum healing to occur. Simple ways to do this are to rest, relax and think happy thoughts. As soon as you think fearful or angry thoughts … the body shifts into a sympathetic stance."

Our consideration of the biological foundations of hatred, grounded as that secondary emotion is in the primary emotions of fear and anger, leads us to conclude that hatred is catabolic or unhealthy to ourselves.

Hate, in fact, operates to tear down and destroy our bodies. At the inter-personal and societal levels, it also tears down and destroys, otherwise potentially cooperative, productive, and satisfying, social relationships.

As Madeline L'Engle has aptly remarked, "Hate hurts the hater more'n the hated." Similarly, Eric Jerome Dickey wrote "hate isn't healthy, it damages the hater more than the one who's hated!" And, finally, "Allow enemies their space to hate; they will destroy themselves in the process," wrote Lisa Du.

More on the Primary and Secondary Emotions

Having considered the biological bases of hate, we return briefly to our discussion of Theodore Kemper's theoretical framework incorporating the primary and secondary emotions and their interrelationships.

Kemper proceeded to discuss how the emergence of the secondary emotions of guilt, pride, and shame may be understood in terms of his analyses (1987, pp. 276-282). Hate was hypothesized by Kemper to be attached to the primary emotions of fear and anger.

If Kemper was correct in his reasoning then, considering his arguing for the central role of the power and status social inequality variables, drawing upon common sense and down-to-earth sociology, you and I may deduce two important hypotheses.

Specifically, our hypotheses are that hate is likely to emerge as a secondary emotion in those situations that are:

1. characterized by interaction outcomes where actors are subject to the power of others because that power is greater than their own (which elicits the primary emotion of fear); and/or

2. where interaction outcomes in which expected, customary, or deserved status has been withdrawn or denied by another actor who is seen to be responsible for the reduced status (which elicits the primary emotion of anger).

Are we good, or what? What a team!

As you will see in chapters 5 and 6, these hypotheses have received both indirect and direct confirmation from the findings of research on hate groups, including my own research.

Kemper's efforts to describe secondary emotions as evolved adaptations involving the primary emotions and the socio-cultural environment complements research on "The CAD Hypothesis: A Mapping Between Three Moral Emotions (Contempt, Anger, Disgust) and Three Moral Codes (Community, Autonomy, Divinity)," by P. Rozin, L. Lowrey, S. Imada, and J. Haidt (1999, pp. 574-586).

Incidentally, although Kemper does not include 'disgust' among the primary emotions, others have, such as leading neuroscientist Antonio Damasio in his book, *The Feeling of What Happens: Body and Emotions in the Making of Consciousness* (2000).

In the next chapter, we shall see that fear, anger, and disgust figure prominently in an important psycho-sociological theory of hate, a theory that strongly bridges the psychology of hate and the sociology of hate.

Meanwhile, if you would like to learn more about the psychology of hate, I recommend that you begin by reading *The Psychology of Hate*, edited by Robert J. Sternberg (2005). Among the topics considered are, for example, "roots of hate, violence, and evil;" "hate, conflict, and moral exclusion;" "genocidal hatred;" and "understanding and combating hate."

CHAPTER 3
The Duplex Theory of Hate, the Unifying Bridge Between The Psychology of Hate and the Sociology of Hate

Recall from our discussion, in the immediately preceding chapter, Theodore Kemper's distinction between the primary and secondary emotions as providing an important bridge between the psychology of hate and the sociology of hate, while also considering the biological foundations of hate in the body's autonomic nervous system.

As I have conducted extensive reviews of the literature on the psychology of hate over the past several years, I have found the research and theoretical contributions of former President of the American Psychological Association, Robert J. Sternberg, to be especially relevant and helpful in linking the psychology of hate and the sociology of hate (2003, 2005, 2008).

Of particular importance to our present purposes is Sternberg's "A Duplex Theory of Hate: Development and Application to Terrorism, Massacres, and Genocide" (2003). As suggested by the title, the duplex theory of hate consist of two closely interrelated parts. The first of these is "The Triangular Theory of the Structure of Hate," while the second is "A Story-Based Theory of the Development of Hate."

While the triangular theory emphasizes the psychological aspects of hate, the story-based theory highlights the importance of hate's sociological side.

The Triangular Theory of the Structure of Hate

For Robert J. Sternberg, hate is most usefully described and analyzed metaphorically (not strictly geometrically) in terms of the vertices of a *triangle* or triangles involving three components; namely, Negation of Intimacy (comprised of the primary emotion of *disgust*), Passion (based upon the primary emotions of *anger/fear*), and Commitment (devaluation/diminution), reflecting the human cognitive or mental states, as opposed to the strictly emotional components of hate (2003, p. 307; 2008, p. 60).

From high school geometry, you may recall that the vertices of a triangle are the corners where the straight lines connect with one another. In Sternberg's hate triangles, Negation of Intimacy, which he abbreviates with the symbol −I, appears at the top of the triangle. Passion, P, shows up at the bottom left, and Commitment, C, at the bottom right.

Interestingly, Sternberg's Duplex Theory of Hate, including both the Triangular and the Story – Based portions of the theory, evolved, more or less naturally, from his earlier "A Triangular Theory of Love" and his "Love is a Story" (1984, 1986, 1994, 1998, 1998b, 2001, 2006).

Love may also be pictured in the form of triangles. In the case of love, there is Intimacy (I), once again at the top of the triangle, Passion, (P), at the bottom on the left, and Commitment (C) at the bottom right.

Of course, the Passion (P) in love is not fear and/or anger, but rather "the drives that lead to romance, physical attraction, sexual consummation, and related phenomena in loving relationships" (2008, p. 54). Similarly, the Commitment (C) component of love refers not to devaluation and diminution, but instead "in the short-term, to the decision that one loves a certain other, and in the long-term, to one's commitment to maintain that love" (2008, p. 55).

As the former President of the American Psychological Association and Karin Sternberg informed us in their co-authored 2008 book, *The Nature of Hate*, regarding the relationships between love and hate:

> ... hate is very closely related psychologically to love. People have always suspected there is some kind of a relation between hate and love. For example, love can rapidly turn to hate. A husband or wife returns early from work and finds his or her spouse in a compromising position. Feelings of love can be replaced, or more likely, supplemented, quickly and overwhelmingly by feelings of hate. The spouse need not even necessarily misbehave to engender feelings of hate. Suspicion of misbehavior can be just as powerful in generating feelings of hate. In general, it is not actions that produce hatred, but, rather, perceptions of those actions (2008, p. 51).

As we shall see in subsequent sections involving the sociology of hate, Sternberg's insistence on the importance of perceptions, which may be distorted by false beliefs and prejudicial attitudes, is of vital importance in understanding both the psychology of hate and the sociology of hate and their close relationships to one another.

The Sternbergs have also written that:

> ... hate is neither the opposite nor the absence of love. Rather, the relationship between love and hate is multifaceted. Love and hate both have three components, which are interrelated. In one case, the components are inverses of each other. In the other case, they are actually the same, but are experienced differently. Different people have different combinations of these

components, so, structurally, may experience hate (or love) differently (2008, pp. 51-52).

These observations by the Sternbergs assume special importance, because they remind us that, despite the social uniformities that unite people in terms of their values, beliefs, attitudes, and behaviors *vis-à-vis* love and hate, psychological and personality differences play crucial roles as well.

They continued their analyses of the relationships between hate and love by writing that:

> ... [and this is where the Sternbergs introduce and underscore the necessary and inescapable relationships between the psychology of hate and the sociology of hate, whether self-conscious on their part or not], hate, like love, has its origins in *stories* that character- ize the *target* of the emotion ... How likely hate is to *manifest* itself in action [such as hate crimes or in the ideologies and activities of *hate groups*, both of which are discussed in later sections of this book] depends in large part upon the particular story or stories that give rise to it (*emphases*, whose reasons will become obvious in later sections of this book, are added by me) (2008, p. 52).

Finally,

> ...hate is one precursor, although certainly not the only precursor, of some instances of terrorism, massacres, and genocide... (2008, p.52).

Finally? Well, not quite. Before elaborating further upon Robert J. Sternberg's "The Triangular Theory of the Structure of Hate," we can learn a great deal more from his and Karin Sternberg's research and theoretical work by quoting the following:

> Underlying these claims [quoted above] is a view con-
> sistent with humanistic psychologists such as [Eric]
> Fromm (1992, 2000) and [Abraham] Maslow (1993),
> that love represents human maturity and fulfillment,
> whereas hate represents a perversion of the positive
> possibilities for humankind (2008, p. 52).

By reading this far in my book, you're not surprised by that last quote, are you?

And, as the Sternbergs have emphasized, very importantly, "Hate is not something we are born with — it is something we acquire" (2008, p.52).

As a sociologist, this is where I finally get to interject and introduce the indispensable and irrefutable importance of the sociological perspective in contributing to our more complete understanding of the reasons for and the very nature of hate.

Specifically, we acquire hate by our being exposed to the values, beliefs, and attitudes that are embedded in the stories that are taught and learned by us as individuals in the society and culture by which we are surrounded and in which we live our daily lives.

Among those innumerable stories are those that portray blacks as ignorant and lazy, Jews as greedy, gays and lesbians as sexual perverts, and so on, along with other hate-infused story lines.

The Sternbergs have also helped bridge the psychology of hate and the sociology of hate by offering their astute observations that:

> Sometimes we acquire it as a result of our perceptions
> of the ways in which *others* act toward us. Other times,
> we acquire it as a result of manipulations of our feelings

and cognitions on the part of *governmental, religious,* or other *leaders* (*emphases* added by me) (2008, p.52).

In summary and to reiterate what you and I learned at the beginning of this section, according to the Sternbergs, hate is most usefully described and analyzed in terms of the vertices of a triangle or triangles involving three components; specifically, the Negation of Intimacy (-I) (comprised of the primary emotion of disgust), Passion (P) (based upon the primary emotions of anger/fear), and Commitment (C) (devaluation/diminution), reflecting the cognitive or mental states, as opposed to the strictly emotional components of hate.

The Sternbergs go on to further elaborate upon the triangular component of the duplex theory of hate:

As with love, hate can be captured by both *feelings* triangles and *action* triangles. Feelings may or may not translate themselves into actions, and actions may or may not represent genuine feelings (*emphases*, added by me) (2008, p. 59).

This critically significant observation by the Sternbergs allows, very importantly, for appropriately crafted and targeted interventions through public policy, and through your and my concerted efforts, to reduce both feelings of hate and the likelihood that persons will actually engage in hateful behaviors, such as either committing hate crimes or endorsing, embracing and engaging in the ideologies and activities of hate groups.

Hang on to this thought and its possibilities, please. We shall return to it especially in Chapter 6, *Respect Diversity – Teach Tolerance – Fight Hate!*

Research Validation of The Triangular Theory of Hate

Robert J. Sternberger has developed a Triangular Hate Scale to measure the components of hate (2008, pp. 217-218).

Negation of Intimacy (-I) is measured by respondents' answers to 10 questions of which the following 3 are typical: "I would never knowingly associate with _____," "I do not feel any compassion toward _____," and "I feel that _____ is fundamentally different in a negative way from people like me."

Degree of Passion (P) is determined by answers to 9 questions, such as "I personally feel threatened by _____," "Thinking about _____ makes me feel insecure," "I can sometimes feel my heart beat faster from the rage I feel when I start thinking about _____," and "When I think of _____ I become very angry."

Lastly, the following are examples of the 10 statements developed to measure Commitment (C): "We need to teach our children about the danger of people like _____," "People need to take an active role in speaking out against people like _____," "The fight against _____ is important regardless of possible costs," and "The public should be informed comprehensively about the danger of _____."

Very importantly, The Triangular Hate Scale has been validated by three carefully designed and well-documented studies conducted in both the United States and Germany (Weis, 2006 [now Mrs. Karin Sternberg, proving my well-established adage that "research, especially of the rigorous and independent confirmatory variety, makes the heart grow fonder"]).

The Story-Based Component of the Duplex Theory of the Development of Hate

As previously emphasized by the Sternbergs, hate triangles, taken by themselves, are insufficient for a complete duplex theory of hate, for their very existence is dependent upon accompanying stories, which function to describe the real or imagined characteristics of the target of hate, usually as compared with the perpetrator(s) of hate.

For example, the Nazi propaganda machine pictured Jews as dirty, dark skinned, scheming, greedy, Christ killers, while the "pure" Nordic Aryans were presented as the antithesis, honest, generous, blond and blue-eyed God-fearing Christians.

In the United States, African Americans were and still are described by many whites as biologically, or at least culturally, inferior: ignorant, lazy, irresponsible, and criminal.

These horrendous stories, unsubstantiated by fact, are repeated and reflected (often in subtle ways) by mainstream media in newspapers, magazines, and television and in not so subtle ways on the Internet, often by hate groups, about which we shall have more to say below.

In the Sternberg duplex theory of hate, a typology of common stories of hate is developed, whereby the categories of stories are described in terms of their hypothesized relationships to the triangular components of Negation of Intimacy (-I), Passion (P), and Commitment (C).

These relationships are summarized in a table entitled "Some stories leading to the development of hate and the elements of the triangle of hate they are hypothesized most to incite" (2008, p. 84).

Among the 28 identifiable hate story types and their relationships to hate triangles, for example, are the:

a. "stranger (vs. in-group)" story characterized by a negation of intimacy and by commitment (-I, C). "The more different is the stranger among us, the more readily is the stranger for externalization – that is, to become the object of hate" (2008, p. 85).

b. "impure other (vs. pure in-group)" story, where there is (-I). "The hated enemy is impure or contaminated ... the enemy is trying to spread the contamination ... The euphemism 'ethnic cleansing' may call to mind images of an enemy that needs to be eliminated from a society that would otherwise be pure in much the same way that dirt needs to be eliminated from holy relics" (2008, pp. 85-86), and

c. "enemy of God (vs. servant of God)" story (P, C). Here "The hated enemy is not only your enemy, but also, an enemy of God" (2008, p. 87).

Other common stories are "controller (vs. controlled)" (C); "barbarian (vs. civilized in group)" (-I, P, C); "greedy enemy (vs. financially responsible in-group)" (-I, C); "criminal (vs. innocent party)" (C); "animal pest (vs. human)" (-I, P); and "comic character (vs. sensible in-group)" (C) (2008, pp. 83-95).

In their The Nature of Hate, the Sternbergs also provided substantial and varied current and historical evidence in support of the theory, and they described its applicability to interpersonal relationships, massacres, terrorism, and genocide.

They also discussed the role of propaganda in inciting hate and combating hate.

You and I owe a great deal to the Sternbergs for their contributions to our understanding of hate.

CHAPTER 4
The Sociology of Hate

The researches and theorizing by contemporary sociologists also complement, expand upon, and in several respects provide evidence supporting various aspects of Sternberg's triangle/story or duplex theory of hate, particularly the story or stories portion of the duplex.

In general, sociologists have studied hate as a social problem, like prejudice and discrimination due to racism, classism, sexism, and ageism, for example, and as a social movement, related and analogous to, but antithetical and reactionary to, the civil rights movement, the women's movement, and the movement for equality for gays, lesbians, bisexual and transgendered people.

Sociologists, as well as criminologists and some political scientists, have focused on a range of hateful cognitive, or mental, and emotional states and behaviors, ranging from values, beliefs, and attitudes evident in the general culture through the more extreme varieties of hate speech and ideologies and behaviors associated with violence or potential violence as manifested in hate crimes and the ideologies and activities of hate groups.

Previous sociological research focused on hate crimes and the ideologies and activities of hate groups have been most directly relevant to my own research on manifest hate.

As numerous sociologists have discovered first-hand, however, observing and recording the ideologies, and especially, the behaviors of individual members of hate groups can be, and usually are, daunting, if not downright discouraging and potentially dangerous. I'll bet that you're not surprised by this revelation, are you?

Sociologist Kathleen Blee's experiences in attempting to study white supremacist groups are typical:

> Gathering accurate information about members of organized racist groups is difficult. Racist activists tend to be disingenuous, secretive, intimidating to researchers, and prone to give evasive or dishonest answers. Standard interviews [often used in other social contexts with success by sociologists] are often unproductive, yielding little more than organizational slogans repeated as personal beliefs (2004, p. 50).

Blee's own response to such challenges to research methodology was to use a life-history approach to learn about the role(s) that women play in hate groups, which allowed her to elicit "from each woman an unstructured account of her life story rather than asking questions about beliefs or commitments ... [and] at the conclusion of the life narratives, I asked each woman a series of open-ended but structured questions to collect comparable background data on individuals and their groups" (2004, pp. 50-51).

It seems likely that women members of hate groups would be somewhat less intimidating to a research sociologist like Kathleen Blee than men haters would be, don't you think?

Complementing these research techniques, were Blee's "observation of racist events ... [and] analysis of documents published and/or distributed by racist groups" (2004, p. 49).

In fact, most of what we know about hate groups, in addition to what is available from researching FBI hate crime data, comes from ethnographic research; life-histories; face-to-face and telephone interviews using structured and unstructured questionnaires; study of the contents of books, articles and pamphlets by hate groups and their leaders; observations of activities such as rallies, marches, speeches, and protests; and reviewing the increasingly numerous "cyber-hate" web sites and messages posted on the Internet and chat room discussions.

Taken altogether, studies of hate crimes and active hate groups have produced a number of important findings, several of which led to the development of useful typologies as well as testable hypotheses evidencing varying degrees of support from relevant research evidence.

Political scientist and sociologist, Chip Berlet, Senior Researcher for the Political Research Associates (PRA), which monitors and tracks hate groups, for example, in his "Mapping the Political Right: Gender and Race Oppression in Right-Wing Movements," has argued that "Bigotry and prejudice are easy to find in the texts of various right-wing movements in the United States, but they occur in varying degrees in different groups and can change over time" (2004, p. 19).

Berlet, very helpfully, proceeded to develop a typology of the right-wing in the United States, which he locates as representing distinguishing sectors on a continuum ranging from the "Conservative Right" near the center of the liberalism-conservatism political dimension to the "Populist Dissident Right," and then to the extreme "Racist Extreme Right."

The Conservative Right, involving politicians, elections and legislation, engages in "reform-oriented political movements" as pursued by the "Republican Party, Heritage Foundation, Federalist Society, Cato Institute, [and the] American Enterprise Institute."

The Populist Dissident Right is involved with "reform-oriented social movements." Among these are Economic Libertarians; Anti-Affirmative Action, Anti-Welfare, Anti-Abortion, Anti-Gay, Anti-Immigrant, and Anti-Statist Tax Revolt groups; Isolationists; Christian Nationalists; and Patriots and Armed Militias.

Finally, groups comprising the Racist Extreme Right are described as pursuing "insurgent social movements." Examples are the White Aryan Group, the Resistance Church of the Creator, Racist Skinheads, Posse Comitatus, Christian Identity, National Alliance, Ku-Klux Klan, and Neo-Nazis (2004, p. 23).

Berlet further elaborated upon his typology by writing that:

> The term extreme right refers to militant insurgent
> groups that reject democracy, promote a conscious

ideology of white supremacy, and support policies that would negate basic humans rights for members of a scapegoated group.

The terms extreme right and racist right are often use interchangeably, although for some groups on the extreme right gender is also a major focus, and racism exists in various forms and degrees in all sectors ...

Furthermore, and oh-so-sadly,

Extreme right ideologies of overt white supremacy and anti-Semitism envision a United States based on unconstitutional forms of discrimination. Extreme right groups are implicitly insurgent because they 'reject the existing political system and pluralist institutions generally, in favor of some form of authoritarianism' ...

Also,

In contrast, dissident-right [as opposed to extreme-right] groups still hope for the reform of the existing system, even when their reforms are drastic and the dissidents are skeptical that their goals will be reached...

Lastly,

The term 'hate group' describes an organization in any sector that overtly and aggressively demonizes or dehumanizes members of a scapegoated target group in a systematic way (2004, p. 22)

Berlet has also argued that "particular styles of expressing ideology are used in creating collective-action frames used by movements to mobilize support."

The most frequently discernible styles are in many ways consistent with the stories identified by psychologist Robert Sternberg in his duplex-theory of hate, such as, the "stranger (vs. in-group)" story, the "impure other (vs. pure in-group)" story, the "enemy of God (vs. servant of God)" story, and the "controller (vs. controlled)" story, for example.

According to Berlet, the following styles are utilized by the conservative right in articulating its ideologies:

- Dualism … a form of binary thinking that divides the world into good versus evil, with no middle ground tolerated. There is no acknowledgment of complexity, nuance, or ambiguity in debates, and hostility is expressed toward those who suggest coexistence, toleration, pragmatism, compromise, or mediation. Dualism generates three related processes: demonization, scapegoating, and conspiracism. Demonizing or scapegoating a subordinated 'Other' is one way to defend white male privilege.

- An Apocalyptic Style … A handful of people have been given a warning so they can make appropriate preparations. Apocalyptic … social movements often combine demonization, scapegoating, and conspiracism with a sense that time is running out, so quick action is needed.

- Conspiracism … is a particular narrative form of scapegoating that frames demonized enemies as part of a vast insidious plot against the common good, while it valorizes the scapegoater as a hero for sounding the alarm.

- Apocalyptic conspiracism across the hard right is a masculinist narrative that engenders confrontation … (2004, p. 24).

Berlet has described the last two narrative styles of right-wing movements in the United States as follows:

- Populist Antielite Rhetoric… The central motif of many right-wing dissident movements is a form of populist antielitism that portrays the current government regime as indifferent, corrupt, or traitorous. These episodes of right-wing populism are often generated by economic, social, or cultural stress that assists right-wing organizers in the mass mobilization of alienated cross-class sectors of a population.

+ Populism plays different chords in each sector of the right – but the recurring melody is a particular form called producerism.

+ Producerist narratives portray a noble middle class of hardworking producers being squeezed by a conspiracy involving parasitic elites above and lazy, sinful, and subversive parasites below …

+ Authoritarian Assertion of Dominance… refers to the relative perceived need for authoritarian enforcement of hierarchical and hegemonic control. Dominance involves both power and privilege… The justification for asserting dominance is frequently based on the self-perceived supremacy of the group making the assertion.

+ This supremacy can be articulated in biological or cultural terms… (2004, pp. 24-25).

It is difficult to overestimate or exaggerate the extreme importance of Chip Berlet's contributions to our understanding of dissident and extreme right-wing groups, including hate groups, and his work has profoundly influenced my own approach to the study of manifest hate.

Berlet further elaborates upon his typology of the conservative right by differentiating among the three sectors in terms of their primary and secondary targets, their operative methodologies, and their major styles (2004, pp. 26-47).

For the Extreme Right movement sector, the primary target is race, while the secondary targets are government and gender. This sector engages in insurgencies of exclusion of and violence against the target(s). Its major styles, listed in order of hypothetical importance are domination, conspiracism, apocalypticism, and populist anitelitism.

The government is the primary target of the Patriot Movement and Armed Militias of the Dissident Right, while gender and race are secondary targets. Reform through defensive vigilantism is the strategy characterizing this sector, with its major styles being populist antielitism, conspiracism, apocalypticism, and domination.

For the Christian Right sector of the Dissident Right, gender is the primary target, with government and race being secondary. This sector pursues its sought for reforms through the electoral process and regulatory measures, through the styles of apocalypticism, conspiracism, domination, and populist antielitism.

Watchdog Organizations

Nationwide monitoring of right-wing dissident and extreme right groups has been a principal preoccupation of watchdog non-governmental organizations, such as the Anti-Defamation League (ADL), the Political Research Associates (PRA), and the Southern Poverty Law Center (SPLC).

Another informative source on "Hate Groups on the Internet" has been compiled by Raymond A. Franklin. His The Hate Directory is available online. If you visit his website, you are likely to be quite astonished to discover, as I did, that its 170 pages list well over 3000 hate group websites, mailing lists, racists games, radio stations, and so on, a clear indication that hate is, depressingly and sadly, alive, well, and thriving in our world.

Depressing? Absolutely. You and I should not be discouraged, however. Even though the challenges to our attaining our shared goals of "Respect Diversity – Teach Tolerance – Fight Hate!" are formidable, we are united by a force that is stronger, far stronger than hate, namely that of love and its close companion, compassion. Adding our shared commitments to reason, research-based knowledge, and a tenacity born of the absolute rightness of our cause makes us an adversary that cannot be defeated.

The ADL was founded in 1913 with the essence of its mission being expressed thusly: "The immediate object of the League is to stop, by appeals to reason and conscience and, if necessary, by appeals to law, the defamation of the Jewish people. Its ultimate purpose is to secure justice and fair treatment to all citizens alike and to put an end forever to unjust and unfair discrimination against and ridicule of any sect, or body, of citizens."

The PRA, which has been existence since 1981, has a mission "... devoted to supporting movements that are building a more just and inclusive democratic society. We expose movements, institutions, and ideologies that undermine human rights." The goal of the PRA is "... to advance progressive thinking and action by providing research-based information, analysis, and referrals."

The websites of both the ADL and PRA contain abundant information useful for recognizing, understanding, and opposing the several varieties of hate groups that are active in the United States today.

A similar function is provided by the SPLC. Founded in 1971, the Southern Poverty Law Center is a well-funded non-profit civil rights organization whose mission is threefold.

It has vigorously pursued lawsuits intended to protect the rights of "exploited workers, abused prison inmates, and other victims of discrimination," and has actually totally and completely bankrupted and put out of business "some of the nation's most violent white supremacist groups." It has been especially aggressive in this regard.

Through its Teaching Tolerance Program, the SPLC also "produces and distributes – free of charge – documentary films, books, lesson plans and other materials that promote tolerance and respect in our nation's schools."

My wife, Nancy, has personally used SPLC Teaching Tolerance Program materials in the classroom, and she has been most impressed by the quality and effectiveness of the materials provided.

The SPLCs third mission component and principal area of activity is that which bears directly on the primary purpose of my own research on manifest hate, which I have been conducting for the past several years. Specifically, the SPLC actively monitors on a daily basis the activities of hate groups throughout the United States.

Developing my Original Sociological Measure of Manifest Hate for my Own Research

From the perspective of my discipline, sociology, where the units of research analysis are often not individuals per se, but rather social groups of varying size and complexity, the measurement of hate can particularly challenging.

How, indeed, can you and I measure manifest hate at the level of, say, nations or subdivisions within them, such as the U.S. states, in a manner that might be useful, through our shared common sense understanding and commitments to down-to-earth sociology, in helping us better to understand the how and why of manifest hate?

In the United States, for example, we find that state level data on hate crimes, which are routinely gathered and published by the FBI in its Uniform Crime Reports (and in other publications), are readily available, and they are easily accessed by you and me.

The validity and reliability of hate crime statistics as measures or indicators of manifest hate are questionable for two primary reasons, however:

(1st) hate crimes tend to be seriously underreported, especially for certain categories of victims, such as gay, lesbian, bisexual, and transgendered (GLBT) persons; and

(2nd) many attitudes, beliefs and behaviors that might be reasonably characterized as hateful and harmful to victims are not considered hate crimes, per se, but are, in fact protected under the free-speech clause of the First Amendment to the *U.S. Constitution*.

Such attitudes, beliefs and behaviors may be inferred from or directly observed in books, newspapers, magazines, pamphlets, and on the Internet; or at speeches, rallies, demonstrations and marches, for example.

The activity of hate groups within states constitutes a data source used by several sociologists, myself included.

In that regard, I have found the "Year in Hate" series of articles appearing annually in each spring issue of the Southern Poverty Law Center (SPLC) *Intelligence Report* to be an excellent source of valid and reliable data for my own research on manifest hate.

The SPLC Monitoring of Hate Groups and Its *Intelligence Report*

In 1981, the SPLC launched Klanwatch, an initiative designed to monitor the activities of the Ku Klux Klan throughout the United States. By 1998, the goal of Klanwatch had been expanded to include the monitoring of other hate groups, and it was given a new name, the Intelligence Project.

The winter 1998, issue of the SPLCs *Intelligence Report* detailed a count of 474 active hate groups in 1997, of which 127 were Klan chapters and Klan organizations, 100 were Neo-Nazi, 42 were Skinheads, 81 Christian Identity, 12 Black Separatist, and 112 described as following "a hodgepodge of hate-based doctrines and ideologies" (1998, p. 89).

The SPLC defines hate groups as having "… beliefs or practices that attack or malign an entire class of people, typically for their immutable characteristics."

Lists of hate groups are compiled "…using hate group publications and websites, citizen and law enforcement reports, field sources and news reports."

While websites are utilized to identify and locate hate groups, "websites appearing to be merely the work of a single individual, rather than the publication of a group, are not included in the list," and being included on the hate group list "does not imply a group advocates or engages in violence or other criminal activity."

Furthermore, "Hate group activities can include criminal acts, marches, rallies, speeches, leafleting or publishing."

By the time the spring 2009 issue of the *Intelligence Report* was published, showing a state-by-state map identifying the location and number of active hate groups in 2008, the total number of such groups had grown to 926, an increase of 95% over the 11 year period.

The hate groups comprising the 926 total were classified by the SPLC into the following categories: Ku Klux Klan with 186 groups; Neo-Nazi, 196; White Nationalist, 111; Racist Skinhead, 98; Christian Identity, 39; Neo-Confederate, 93; Black Separatist, 113; and General Hate, 90 (Holthouse 2009, pp. 48-69).

The total number of hate groups increased by an additional 6 in 2009, bringing the new total to 932, as reported in the spring 2010 issue of the *Intelligence Report*.

My Newly-Developed State Hate Index (SHI) as a Measure of Manifest Hate, Based Upon the SPLC Monitoring of Hate Groups and a Common Sense and Down-to-Earth Sociology Ratio

The SPLC annual reports on the numbers of hate groups, appearing in each spring issue of the *Intelligence Report*, contain actual and detailed state-by-state lists of hate groups active throughout the immediately preceding year.

If you visit their website, be sure to click on the "HATE MAP" link, where you can find the active hate groups in your state, including their geographic locations, in some cases.

For the year 2010, for example, there were a total of 1002 hate groups identified, documented, classified and enumerated by the research staff of the SPLC's Intelligence Project, the largest number ever recorded for any single "Year in Hate."

If these hate groups had been distributed equally among the 50 U.S. states and Washington, D.C., each of the 51 would be expected to have 19.65 active hate groups (1002 ÷ 51).

The hate groups were anything other than equally distributed among the states and D.C., however, with a range extending from the 68 counted in California to 0 found in both Alaska and Hawaii.

Closest to California was Texas with its 59 hate groups, while Rhode Island, South Dakota and Vermont each had 2 only.

Near the middle of the distribution were Arkansas, Illinois and Virginia, each of which had 29 active hate groups in 2010.

Sociologists, including myself, rascals that we are, tend to be skeptical of simple actual numbers, however, especially when they are associated with ecological/geographical units of analysis, such as the U.S. states.

Here is where we once again demonstrate the usefulness of down-to-earth sociology linked with common sense.

For example, it is possible that the reason California had the highest number of hate groups might be due to the fact that it also had the largest total population of any state in 2010, approximately 37 million people. Similarly, maybe Alaska had no hate groups simply because it was among the least populated states, with its 2010 population of only 698,473.

The most common approach used by sociologists to "control" for potential biases caused by differences in population sizes is to calculate ratios and rates, such sex ratios, birth rates, death rates, marriage rates, obesity rates, smoking rates, teen pregnancy rates, suicide rates, murder rates, prison incarceration rates, and so forth.

If you read my recent book, *Economic Inequality and What YOU Can Do About It: A Primer and Call to Action!*, you will recall that I made extensive use of ratios in contributing to our understanding of various aspects of income and wealth inequality in the United States.

A ratio is one of the easiest and useful descriptive statistics to understand. It is simply one number divided by another, as in a ÷ b. For example, imagine that while you are reading this book, 900 other people across the United States are enjoying it as well. Would I be lucky, or what? My, oh my, oh yes. Certainly, I would be most happy and grateful if it were true.

Imagine further that of the 900 readers, 500 were men and 400 were women. The ratio of male readers to female readers would therefore be 500 ÷ 400 = 1.25, meaning that for every 1 female reader there were 1.25 male readers.

Oftentimes, ratios are multiplied by 100, so that in the case of our current example, we can say that for every 100 female readers there were 125 male readers.

Incidentally, the ratio of males to females is referred to as the sex ratio, and it is frequently used by sociologists and other social scientists to study the composition of human populations at all levels, such as city, county, state, region, and nation.

For example, according to the United States Census Bureau, there were 151,781,326 males counted in the 2010 Census and 156,964,212 females. The sex ratio for 2010 was, therefore,

151,781,326 ÷ 156,964,212 = .97. Multiplied by 100, we observe that for every 100 females there were 97 males.

The State Hate Index (SHI) that I have developed as the measure of manifest hate for my own research is also a simple ratio to calculate and understand.

My SHI is simply the ratio of a state's percentage share of the nation's total number of hate groups divided by that state's percentage share of the total U.S. population. For example, in 2010 California had 6.8% of the nation's active hate groups and 12.04% of the U.S. population, so that its SHI for that year was .56 = (6.8% ÷ 12.04%).

One of the most important characteristics of the SHI that renders it especially useful for making comparisons between and among states is that, when a state's percentage share of the nation's hate groups equals its share of the U.S. population, the SHI assumes the value of 1.00.

That being the case, therefore, we can reason that hate groups were actually "underrepresented" in California in 2010, even though it actually had the largest number of hate groups. Its SHI of .56 means that it had only a bit more than half, 56%, of the number of hate groups that it might have had, based on the size of its population.

The cases of Arkansas, Illinois and Virginia, illustrate even more dramatically how my SHI can better describe inter-state differences in what I call manifest hate, than the actual numbers of hate groups counted for each state.

While Arkansas, Illinois and Virginia each had 29 hate groups in 2010, their SHIs were 3.06, 0.70 and 1.12, respectively, leading us to be able to assert, for example, that while Arkansas had 2.06 times more than its "fair share" (based on its population size) of hate groups, Illinois had only 70% of what it could have had, while Virginia was very close to having its "fair share of 1.0" with an SHI of 1.12.

The State Hate Index (SHI), applied to the 50 U.S. states and Washington, D.C., is the operationally defined sociological measure or indicator utilized to examine relationships between manifest hate and a wide variety of other social problems for my research on manifest hate in the United States.

Since the most recent year for which most of the other related relevant social problems data of my research, whose findings I present for your information and consideration in the next chapter, are directly comparable is 2008, the 2008 SHI is the starting point for our analyses.

My State Hate Index (SHI) Values for 2008, 2009, and the 2008-2009 SHI Average

As noted above, altogether, the SPLC identified 626 hate groups active during 2008, that number increasing by 6 to 632 for 2009 (Potok 2010).

The net increase of 6 reflected notable variations in the specific year-to-year differences for the 50 states and D.C., however, with some degree of accompanying changes in the SHIs.

While for 36 states the two-year differences in the numbers of active hate groups ranged between − 3 and + 3, several others exhibited larger variation, the most extreme instance being that of California with its 84 hate groups for 2008 decreasing by 24 to 60 for 2009. The largest increase for any state was the jump of 9 for Iowa, from 8 to 17.

Since I am by nature a cautious person, sometimes to the point of obsessive compulsivity, and in the interest of maximizing the reliability and validity of my measure of manifest hate, the State Hate Index (SHI), it seemed most prudent to utilize the two-year average of the SHIs as the indicator of manifest hate for the 51 units of my research analysis; namely the 50 U.S. States and Washington, D.C.

Table 1 displays the numbers of active hate groups for 2008 and 2009 in the first two data columns, the two-year numerical differences in the third, the 2008 and 2009 SHIs in columns four and five, respectively, and the two-year SHI average, as SHI0809, in the sixth column.

Table 1: Numbers of Active Hate Groups for 2008 and 2009, the Two-Year Differences, the State Hate Index (SHI) Values for 2008 and 2009, and the Two-Year SHI Averages, SHI0809.

State	Hate Groups in 2008	Hate Groups in 2009	Two Year Difference 2009 – 2008	SHI 2008	SHI 2009	Two Year Average SHI0809
AL	36	32	-4	2.58	2.24	2.41
AK	0	1	1	0	0.47	0.235
AZ	19	16	-3	0.99	0.8	0.895
AR	20	24	4	2.32	2.74	2.53
CA	84	60	-24	0.76	0.53	0.645
CO	15	17	2	1.02	1.11	1.065
CT	5	6	1	0.47	0.56	0.515
DC	8	9	1	4.53	4.94	4.735
DE	4	4	0	1.54	1.49	1.515
FL	56	51	-5	1.01	0.91	0.96
GA	40	37	-3	1.38	1.24	1.31
HI	0	1	1	0	0.25	0.125
ID	7	9	2	1.55	1.92	1.735
IL	23	28	5	0.59	0.71	0.65
IN	16	17	1	0.84	0.87	0.855
IA	8	17	9	0.88	1.86	1.37
KS	8	6	-2	0.94	0.7	0.82
KY	11	10	-1	0.86	0.76	0.81
LA	22	28	6	1.7	2.05	1.875
ME	1	2	1	0.26	0.5	0.38
MD	13	13	0	0.76	0.75	0.755
MA	13	16	3	0.66	0.8	0.73
MI	23	26	3	0.75	0.86	0.805
MN	8	9	1	0.51	0.56	0.535
MS	22	25	3	2.51	2.79	2.65
MO	30	31	1	1.69	1.71	1.7
MT	6	12	6	2.1	4.05	3.075
NE	4	4	0	0.74	0.73	0.735
NV	13	15	2	1.67	1.87	1.77
NH	3	5	2	0.74	1.24	0.99
NJ	40	44	4	1.52	1.66	1.59
NM	1	2	1	0.17	0.33	0.25
NY	24	31	7	0.41	0.52	0.465
NC	30	29	-1	1.05	1.02	1.035
ND	1	1	0	0.52	0.51	0.515
OH	23	27	4	0.66	0.77	0.715
OK	19	15	-4	1.74	1.34	1.54

OR	7	10	3	0.62	0.86	0.74
PA	37	28	-9	0.84	0.73	0.785
RI	2	3	1	0.63	0.94	0.785
SC	45	36	-9	3.38	2.6	2.99
SD	4	3	-1	1.65	1.22	1.435
TN	38	37	-1	2.04	1.94	1.99
TX	66	66	0	0.91	0.88	0.895
UT	5	6	1	0.62	0.71	0.665
VT	2	1	-1	1.1	0.53	0.815
VA	26	22	-4	1.12	0.92	1.02
WA	12	15	3	0.62	0.74	0.68
WV	14	13	-1	2.56	2.35	2.455
WI	10	8	-2	0.59	0.47	0.53
WY	2	4	2	1.29	2.42	1.855
Totals	926	932	6			

Sources: R. Georges Delamontage. 2012. "Relationhsips between Varieties of Religious Experience and Manifest Hate: A Sociologicsl Analysis." *Journal of Religion and Society*, 14: 1-25. Available online at: http://moses.creighton/JRS/2012/2012-23.pdf.
The numbers of active hate groups in 2008 and 2009 are from David Holthouse, "The Year Hate" (2009) and Mark Potok "The Year in Hate" (2010) iin the Spring 2009 and 2010 issu respectively, of the Southern Poverty Law Center (SPLC) *Intelligence Report*.

Like the tables found in my recent book on economic inequality, I hope that you will find this one to be quite straightforward, easy to understand and interpret, and, even interesting. I can only hope.

Let's start by looking at the very first state in the table, where all states are listed alphabetically according to their U.S. Postal Service abbreviation designations (AK for Arkansas, CT for Connecticut, IA for Iowa, etc.). Alabama (AL) had 36 active hate groups in 2008, with that number decreasing to 32 in 2009. The third column shows the 2009 minus 2008 difference to be − 4, meaning that there were 4 fewer active hate groups in Alabama in 2009 than there were in 2008.

Alabama's State Hate Index (SHI) for 2008 is displayed in the table's 4th column as 2.58, which means that Alabama had 1.58 times more hate groups than you and I would have predicted based on the size of its population.

From looking at the 5th column, we learn that Alabama's SHI dropped to 2.34, and from the 6th column that the average of the 2008 and 2009 SHIs, the SHI0809, is 2.41.

By way of contrast, and to take another example, let's take a look at the same data for the State of Utah (UT).

Utah had 5 active hate groups in the 2008 column 1, that number increasing to 6 in column 2. Its SHI correspondingly increased from .62 in 2008 to .71 in 2009, with the SHI0809 of the last column being .665. Utah, therefore, had a lower SHI than we would have predicted based on its population size; namely, it had 66% as many as it could have had if its SHI had been 1.0.

By way of further contrast, let's examine the same data for our nation's capital, Washington, D.C.

For D.C., we can see that it had 8 active hate groups in 2008 and 9 in 2009, its corresponding SHIs for those years being 4.53 and 4.94, the very highest SHIs for any political jurisdiction in the country.

Is this a disgraceful contrast, or what?

Looking at the last column of our table, we observe that D.C.s two year average was 4.735, meaning, or course that it had 3.735 times more active hate groups than you and I would have predicted from knowing its population size.

If you read my recent book, *Economic Inequality and What YOU Can Do About It: A Primer and Call to Action!*, you may remember that I devoted a substantial section, which I labeled as A Note on a Recurring Statistical Outlier, the Disturbing Case of Washington, D.C. in Chapter 8.

Your and my concern in that book was Washington D.C.s extreme degree of income inequality, as compared with the 50 U.S. states, and the reality that it also had the highest rates on a variety of measures of social problems or indicators of societal dysfunction, such as the highest violent crime and murder rates, the highest child poverty rates, the highest teen pregnancy rates, the highest infant mortality rates, and the lowest average life expectancy rates.

Those findings led us to decide that the "D.C." actually represented the words "Disgraceful Contrasts," and that moniker applies equally well to our nation's capital when it comes to its relative ranking vis-à-vis the 50 U.S. states in terms of its proportional representation of active hate groups, the SHIs.

What an embarrassing and shameful reality. You and I should immediately contact our elected U.S. senators and representatives, bring these economic and manifest hate realities to their attention, and absolutely demand that they take any and all corrective actions to solve these disgraceful social problems!

In Table 2, I present the 50 U.S. states and Washington, D.C., rank-ordered from the highest to the lowest value on the SHI0809s. In Table 2, and throughout the remainder of this book, I refer to the SHI0809 by the simpler, more succinct, and more easily understood descriptor, the HATE RATE.

Table 2: HATE RATES for the 50 U.S. States and Washington, D. C., 2008- 2009.

State	HATE RATE
D.C.	4.735
MT	3.075
SC	2.99
MS	2.65
AR	2.53
WV	2.455
AL	2.41
TN	1.99
LA	1.875
WY	1.855
NV	1.77
ID	1.735
MO	1.7
NJ	1.59
OK	1.54
DE	1.515
SD	1.435
IA	1.37
GA	1.31
CO	1.065
NC	1.035
VA	1.02
NH	0.99
FL	0.96
AZ	0.895
TX	0.895
IN	0.855
KS	0.82
VT	0.815
KY	0.81
MI	0.805
PA	0.785
RI	0.785
MD	0.755
OR	0.74
NE	0.735
MA	0.73
OH	0.715
WA	0.68
UT	0.665
IL	0.65

CA	0.645
MN	0.535
WI	0.53
CT	0.515
ND	0.515
NY	0.465
ME	0.38
NM	0.25
AK	0.235
HI	0.125

Source: SHI0809 column of Table 1, above.

Examining the HATE RATE rank-ordered data of Table 2 shows the unique and extreme position of our nation's capital. That table also allows you to find your state and compare its HATE RATE to others.

Are you surprised by where your own state ranks? Why or why not? I would be interested in learning of your findings and reactions at: whenhatehappens@gmail.com.

The data of Table 2 on the HATE RATE figure prominently in my own research on manifest hate, with which I have been actively involved since 2008.

I am more than a little excited about and welcome this opportunity to share the results of my research with you in the next chapter. Lucky me.

My sincere hope, of course, is that you will find the results of my research interesting and that they will help increase and improve your own understanding of manifest hate in the United States and its sad and corrosive effects on our society.

I hope further that you will join me in efforts to "Respect Diversity – Teach Tolerance – Fight Hate!" as discussed in Chapter 6.

PART II

Hate and Other Bad Stuff

CHAPTER 5
Findings from my Own Research on Manifest Hate as Measured by my HATE RATE

Since about 2007, when I first became interested in the subject of manifest hate, I have found that a growing body of social scientific literature bearing upon the matter of the degree of *existential insecurity*, experienced at both the individual and societal levels, showed the greatest promise for most appropriately guiding my own research.

The term 'existential insecurity' refers to the reality that, as human beings, we are all vulnerable and mortal, subject to the threats posed by illness, disease, and potential physical and emotional hurt or harm from bacteria, animals, and even from other people in the natural, biological, and social environments in which we all live.

Being a sociologist through and through, from head to toe, you might say, my particular interest has been on 'existential insecurity' coming from our human environment, including its economic, political, and social dimensions.

Among the most important of these aspects of our day-to-day lives are those that threaten our livelihoods and very ability to stay alive and thrive, including having enough money to provide for our basic needs for food, water, clothing, shelter, health care, education, safety from crime, protection from uncontrolled fire, and so forth.

Ii you read my recent book, *Economic Inequality and What YOU Can Do About It: A Primer and Call to Action!*, you may recall that I introduced you to and recommended that you read Dr. Peter Corning's,

The Fair Society: The Science of Human Nature and the Pursuit of Social Justice.

In that superb and most informative book, Dr. Corning amasses and considers an abundance of verifiable scientific evidence from the study of animal behavior, anthropology, behavioral genetics, the brain sciences, evolutionary psychology, and experimental and behavioral economics, that leads him to advance the following threefold definition of fairness, which he refers to as precepts:

+ Goods and services must be distributed to each of us according to our basic needs (in this, there must be *equality*).

+ Surpluses beyond the provisioning of our basic needs must be distributed according to "merit" (there must also be *equity*).

+ In return, each of us is required to contribute proportionately to the collective survival enterprise in accordance with our ability (there must be *reciprocity*) (2011, p. 154).

Although you and I might be inclined to think of basic needs as including only food, water, clothing and shelter, Dr. Corning actually identifies and scientifically justifies the inclusion of fourteen of them, his list including thermoregulation, waste elimination, nutrition, water, mobility, sleep, respiration, physical safety, physical health, mental health, communications, social relationships, reproduction, and nurturance of offspring (2011, pp. 97-107).

While you really need to read Dr. Corning's book, cover to cover, to grasp fully the meaning of his three precepts of fairness and his explanation of basic needs, I personally believe that his arguments are persuasive and I am confident that you will give them fair consideration, whether you end up agreeing with him or not. It is a very well written book, and it is only about 200 pages long.

The greatest strength of Dr. Corning's position on basic needs and fairness is that it is based upon hard and verifiable scientific data and information, and not simply on personal and numerous off-the-top-of-the-head opinions that can be biased by one's particular political orientation and one's unexamined and unchallenged commitments to unsubstantiated and unverifiable economic, political, or social beliefs.

"Extra" money for entertainment, a vacation, and a few "luxuries," such telephone, television, and a PC or laptop computer, while not absolutely necessary to survival, are generally included by most Americans to be part of the American Dream, in which we all have a hope of or expectation to be included.

To the extent that we lack sufficient life-sustaining access to income, food, water, clothing, housing, health care, education, transportation, police and fire protection, and so forth, we are very likely, in varying degrees, depending upon our own particular circumstances, to feel that our well-being, or very existence, is threatened.

That is precisely what is meant by feelings of 'existential insecurity.'

In my own research, I have focused on existential insecurity caused by a wide variety of potential 'existential stressors,' including those related to economic, educational, ethnic-racial, and gender inequalities

Let's start with the economic stressors that can threaten our existential security.

Existential Insecurity resulting from Economic Stressors and their Effects on Manifest Hate

In their *The Spirit Level: Why Greater Equality Makes Societies Stronger* (2009), epidemiologists Richard Wilkinson and Kate Pickett have provided an abundance of data that support hypotheses predicting that *greater social inequality*, which affects existential insecurity, relates to numerous measures of societal dysfunction or social problems.

The units of analysis for their research were of two types, and the results were largely mutually-supporting.

The first data set involved nation states, with particular emphasis upon the differences among the 20 to 30 or so "rich countries," including the United States, while the second set of units of analysis were the 50 U.S. states.

For both the nations and the U.S. states, Wilkinson and Pickett utilized the Gini Coefficient as the measure of inequality of median household income (existential insecurity).

If you read my recent book, *Economic Inequality and What YOU Can Do About It: A Primer and Call to Action!*, you will recall that the Gini Coefficient is an economic inequality measure of statistical dispersion whose values range from 0 to 1, where a value of 1 is indicative of a situation where all of the income is held by one household or a very small group of households, and a value of 0 is obtained when all of the income is shared equally among all households.

Obviously, the ends of the Gini distribution, 0 and 1, are theoretical extremes that could never exist in reality.

You might be interested to learn that the Gini Coefficient has been used to study inequalities in a wide variety of disciplines, such as sociology, economics, health science, ecology, chemistry, engineering, and agriculture.

It is commonly employed as a measure of inequality of either or both income and wealth, and it was developed by the Italian statistician and sociologist Corrado Gini, who published his work in his 1912 paper, "Variability and Mutability."

The Gini Coefficient is also known as the Gini Index or Gini Ratio, and you are already familiar with the general concept and application of ratios. While its calculation is not as simple as a ÷ b, its interpretation is actually similar in several respects. In this regard, a word of caution is in order, however.

Since a Gini Ratio value cannot be higher than 1.0, nor less than 0, you might be tempted to reason that the mean and median are both about .50, so that only values above .50 would be considered to reflect above average levels of income or wealth inequality. It turns out that, since the Gini Ratio is based on something called the Lorenz Curve, a value of .50 is actually indicative of a relatively high level of economic inequality.

Incidentally, while the calculated Gini Ratio values actually range between 0 and 1.0, sometimes they are presented as though they were percentages; namely, they are multiplied by 100, so that a Gini of .390 would appear as 39%, for example.

One of the major advantages of the Gini Coefficient is that it can be used to compare levels of income or wealth inequality among any number and types of areas, such as states, regions, or countries.

Furthermore, since it can be calculated at any point in time, it can be used to study changes occurring between various years, allowing us to measure, for example, the effects of government policies and/or programs intended to reduce levels of economic inequality.

In 2007, for example, Gini values for the 50 states and the District of Columbia ranged from lows of .4104 and .4151 for Vermont and New Hampshire, states with the lowest levels of income inequality, to highs of .4985 and .5432 for New York State and Washington, D.C., respectively (U.S. Census Bureau, 2008).

Using the Gini Coefficient as the measure of income inequality of median household income for the 50 states, Wilkinson and Pickett, observed the following relationships, each of which was pictured graphically in a scatter diagram where the values of the Gini Coefficient occupied the horizontal or "X" axis: the higher the income inequality, the lower the score on an index of women's status; the higher the income inequality, the lower the life expectancy; the higher the income inequality the higher the infant mortality rate.

Incidentally, and as you will see below, I also displayed the results of my sociological research focused on existential insecurity and manifest hate using scatter diagrams. Relying upon both common sense and basic down-to-earth-sociology statistics, I will assist you in understanding and interpreting scatter diagrams in the next section of this chapter.

Similar correlational relationships with higher inequality were observed by Wilkinson and Pickett in *The Spirit Level* regarding higher obesity rates, lower high school completion rates, higher teen (ages 15-19) birth rates, higher homicide rates and higher prison incarceration rates.

Existential Insecurity from Economic Stressors and their Effects on Manifest Hate

In my *Evolutionary Psychology* article, "High Religiosity and Societal Dysfunction in the United States during the First Decade of the Twenty-First Century" (2010), where the sociological research units of analysis were the 50 states and D.C., I found that the social inequality (existential insecurity) variables of income, education and race better explained inter-state differences in violent crime rates; murder rates; incarceration rates; teen (ages 15-19) birth rates; obesity rates; smoking rates; morbidity, or sickness, rates; and several other indicators of social problems or societal dysfunction than extreme religiosity did.

Arguably, extreme degrees of manifest hate, which increase the likelihood of harm being perpetrated upon the victims of hate, may also be considered a serious social problem.

Incidentally, my *Evolutionary Psychology* article was published under my French pseudonym, R. Georges Delamontagne.

In conducting my research for this book, guided as I was by the previous work of Wilkinson and Pickett in their *The Spirit Level*, among others, such as Pippa Norris and Ronald Inglehart's *Sacred and Secular* (2004), whose work we will consider below, I formulated a series of testable sociological hypotheses.

Within each of my 22 hypotheses, the variable of principal interest was my measure of manifest hate, the HATE RATE, which was explained and discussed in Chapter 4.

I present the results of my hypothesis testing research in the series of 22 hypotheses and associated figures that appear below.

Each hypothesis and associated figure has a number, a title that is intended to summarize its contents, a scatter diagram (that I will attempt to help you understand and interpret), and a new statistic, the correlation coefficient, that I will also try to explain in common sense, as opposed to in mathematical or statistical language, terms.

Let the fun begin with Hypothesis 1 and its associated Figure 1.

Here we go. Climb aboard the common sense and down-to-earth sociology statistics express!

Specifically, and to get the train rolling, so to speak, regarding the relationship between manifest hate and existential insecurity resulting from economic stressors, specifically those relating to income inequality, the first hypothesis I tested was:

Hypothesis 1: The higher the degree of existential insecurity within the United States, as measured by the Gini Coefficient (GINI), the higher the degree of manifest hate, as measured by my HATE RATE.

The results of the test of this hypothesis appear in Figure 1.

Figure 1: Relationship between the Gini Coefficient (GINI) and the HATE RATE for the 50 U.S. States and Washington, D.C.

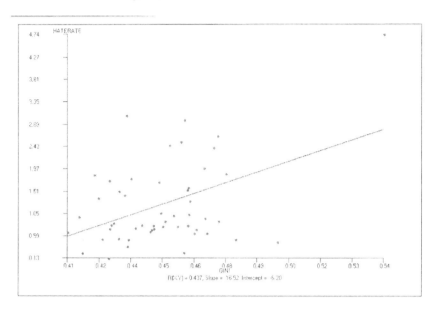

Note: The correlation coefficient, R[X,Y], of .437 is statistically significant at p = .001.

Finding: The higher the degree of income inequality, as measured by the Gini Coefficient, the higher the HATE RATE.

Sources: The 2008/2009 HATE RATE data are from my Table 2, above. 2007 Gini Coefficient data derive from the U.S. Census Bureau (2008).

Explanation of the Scatter Diagram, Note, and Finding:

Scatter Diagram

Regarding the scatter diagram, it has been said, and I'm sure you've heard, that "a picture is worth a thousand words." I'll try to use fewer words than that to explain the scatter diagram, which is the picture that appears in the above box.

For starters, although I often like to pride myself about thinking outside the box, I promise to stay within it, at least for now.

The first two things to focus on are the so-called axes, the horizontal line at the bottom, which is referred to as the X axis, and the vertical line at the left, which is the Y axis.

Characteristically, although not always, the independent variable is displayed on the X or horizontal axis. The independent variable is that which is presumed or hypothesized to have an effect upon the dependent variable which is featured on the Y or vertical axis.

Incidentally, for each of my 22 scatter diagrams, my HATE RATE values are displayed on the Y, or dependent variable, axis. As you review the results of my research, you may encounter several instances where my HATE RATE might have been better presented on the X axis. If you think about it, keep notes about your observations and let me know your thoughts at: whenhatehappens@gmail.com. This is not a test, but it is a challenge. Challenges keep us sharp and delightfully on our toes.

With regard to this figure, Figure 1, the Gini Coefficient, GINI, values are displayed just below the X axis. Observe that they range from a low of .410 on the extreme left to .540 on the extreme right.

Look now at the vertical axis labeled HATE RATE, with which you are already familiar. Those values range from a low of .13 to a high of 4.74.

Now, look inside the box.

Let's start with all of the little dots. There are 51 of them, 50 representing one of 50 U.S. states, and 1 Washington, D.C.

In the Appendix, appearing at the end of the text of this book, you will observe, if you have the patience, the Gini Coefficients and the HATE RATES for the 50 U.S. states and Washington, D.C., so that you can easily locate your state of residence and its associated Gini Coefficient and HATE RATE.

In that Appendix, you can also find the individual state values on all of the 22 existential insecurity variables considered in my research. Are you lucky, or what?

To demonstrate how to interpret the location of a given dot in the scatter-diagram, look up at the upper right hand corner of the box, where you will see what looks like a lost and lonely stranger to the other 50 dots on the sheet.

You might be surprised to learn that that particular dot represents our nation's capital, Washington, D.C. How did get up there to the right, so far away from the others, you ask?

The statistical answer to that question lies in looking at the numbers along both the horizontal axis, X, and the vertical axis, Y. Note, again, that the GINI values are displayed along the X axis, ranging from a low of .41 on the left to a high of .54 on the right. That .54 represents the highest level of income inequality of any jurisdiction in the country.

Look now at the HATERATE, values along the Y axis. The highest rate is 4.74, again describing another disturbing fact about Washington, D.C. We shall have more to say about the shameful and inexcusable reality that is our Washington, D.C., below.

Any other of the 50 states can be located in the box by knowing its GINI and HATERATE values. Again, you can find them in the Appendix, and, with patience, you can locate your own state represented by its dot in the scatter diagram. I strongly encourage you to do so.

Incidentally, dots that stick out, or are far removed from the others are called statistical outliers, Washington, D.C., being a recurring outlier in the figures of this study, as you will see. Just look for the 4.74 HATERATE values on the vertical axis of each scatter diagram and its associated dot in the scatter diagram.

Do you have any ideas as to why D.C. seems to be such an exemplar of both economic inequality and manifest hate?

Think about it. I have, and I would be interested in learning your thoughts on the subject at: whenhatehappens@gmail.com.

What about the line passing more or less through the middle of the dots? It's called the regression line, and you'd have to take my course in sociological statistics for me to explain it to you fully. Alternatively, since I'm happily retired, you'll just have to take that statistics course with someone else. I strongly encourage you to do so.

At this point, suffice it to say that the line is that one of many possible such lines that represents the very "best fit" to all of the dots.

One more thing to note before leaving the regression line is the matter of its slope, which is from the bottom left to the upper right in this particular case. Lines that slope in that direction are said to display a positive relationship between the variables.

A positive relationship between the degree of income inequality, as measured by the Gini Coefficient (GINI), and the HATERATE, means that the higher the Gini Coefficient, the higher the HATERATE.

Sad, maybe, but true, and probably not surprising, when you remember what we discussed earlier about the tendency of high levels of income inequality being related to a wide variety of social problems, as Wilkinson and Pickett also reported in *The Spirit Level.* You're not surprised, are you?

Let's now examine the "R[X,Y] = 0.437, Slope = 16.52, Intercept = −6.20" line at the very bottom of the scatter-diagram box. The slope and intercept are simply values that describe the line mathematically or statistically, and you'd have to take that statistics course to learn how to calculate them. I so very much wish that I could be your professor.

It may sound intimidating, but it's really quite simple and straightforward once you get into it. But, lucky you, we don't have to get into that level of detail for our present purposes.

We do, however, need to discuss the meaning of 'R[X,Y],' making you not quite as lucky as you thought you were, after all.

Who said that life was always or even usually fair, or even sometimes or mostly easy for that matter?

R[X,Y] refers to the correlation coefficient, a simple descriptive statistic that is commonly used to describe the strength and direction of the relationship between two variables.

Although the designation R[X,Y] appears below this particular scatter diagram, and the ones that follow, the correlation coefficient is more commonly presented by simply the small letter 'r,' as in r = .437, for example.

A minus sign in front of the correlation coefficient value, as in −.401 for example, indicates a negative relationship between the variables; namely, the higher the value of X, the lower the value of Y. In such cases, the regression line slopes in the opposite direction, upper left to lower right. We'll see some examples of negative correlations below.

As to all the possible values that r or R[X,Y] may assume, the range is from − 1.0 to 0 to + 1.0, where a 0 means that there is no relationship between the variables and 1.0 designates a perfect relationship between them, − 1.0, when the relationship is negative, and + 1.0, when it is positive.

When R[X,Y] is −1.0 or + 1.0, all of the dots in the scatter diagram line up exactly on the regression line, regardless of the direction of the slope.

When the value of R[X,Y] is 0, the dots are scattered all over the place within the box, so that it becomes very difficult, if not impossible, to place a meaningful regression line. We'll see a few examples of scatter diagrams with R[X,Y]s close to 0 below.

The closer the value of R[X,Y] is to −1.0 or to + 1.0, the stronger is the relationship between the two variables.

Although there are no absolute guidelines to direct us in this regard, ranges of values such as the following can be found in a number of basic sociology statistics textbooks:

Values of the Correlation Coefficient, R[X,Y], and the Strength and Direction of the Relationship Between the two Variables, X and Y.

R[X,Y] Value	Strength and Direction of the Relationship between X and Y
.75 to 1.00	Very strong positive
.50 to .74	Strong positive
.25 to .49	Moderately strong positive
.00 to .24	Weak positive
.00 to - .24	Weak negative
-.25 to -.49	Moderately strong negative
-.50 to -.74	Strong negative
-.75 to -1.00	Very strong negative

Comparing the .437 R[X,Y] we found for the relationship between the Gini Coefficient of income inequality (GINI) and the HATERATE with the ranges of values of the above table, we may infer that there is a moderately strong positive relationship between the variables.

Note

The note appearing immediately below the scatter diagram of Figure 1 reads as follows: "Note: The correlation coefficient, R[X,Y], is statistically significant at p = .001."

The matter of statistical significance is best explained in a basic course in statistics, but all you need to know at this time is that any time you see a "p" value that is equal to or less than .05, you may assume that the associated R[X,Y] is statistically significant, which means simply that the finding is very unlikely to be due to chance alone.

If p = .05, for example, it is safe to presume that there is less than a 5% chance out of 100% that you'll be wrong in inferring that there is, in fact, a relationship between X and Y.

Since most of the findings reported in this book are at levels well below p = .05, you can be quite confident that they are statistically significant.

Speaking of findings, we conclude this section by explaining that particular line appearing under the note beneath the scatter diagram.

You're ready, aren't you? If not, please prepare yourself. It's not a really big deal. Trust me on this, please.

Finding

The finding line below Figure 1 reads "Finding: The higher the degree of income inequality, as measured by the Gini Coefficient, the higher the HATE RATE." This is simply a summary statement of what the information contained within Figure 1 has revealed to us, provided that we have taken the time to examine it carefully and to think about it.

Let's now move on to consider a number of other measures of economic inequality that might be indicative of existential insecurity and also be related to levels manifest hate, as measured by my HATE RATE.

Hypothesis 2: The higher the degree of existential insecurity within the United States, as measured by the Median Household

Income (MDINCOME), the higher the degree of manifest hate, as measured by my HATE RATE.

The results of the test of this hypothesis appear in Figure 2.

Figure 2: Relationship between the Median Household Income (MDINCOME) and the HATE RATE for the 50 U.S. States and Washington, D.C.

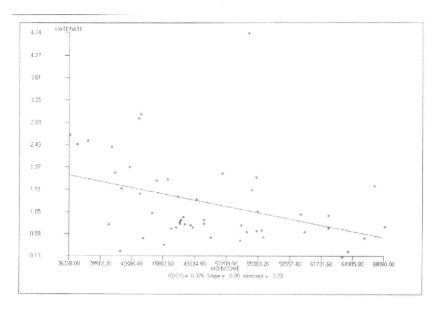

Note: The correlation coefficient, R[X,Y], of −.375 is statistically significant at p = .007. Please observe that the regression line slopes from the upper left to lower right, opposite to that of Figure 1. This type of slope, as we noted earlier, is typical of negative relationships between variables.

Finding: The higher the degree of income inequality, as measured by the Median Household Income, the higher the HATE RATE. This finding may also be stated as follows: the lower the median family income, the higher the HATE RATE, which is what the slope of the regression line portrays.

Sources: The 2008/2009 HATE RATE data are from my Table 2, above. 2007 median household income data derive from the U.S. Census Bureau (2008).

Hypothesis 3: The higher the degree of existential insecurity within the United States, as measured by the poverty rate (POVERTY), the higher the degree of manifest hate, as measured by my HATE RATE.

The results of the test of this hypothesis appear in Figure 3.

Figure 3: Relationship between the Poverty Rate (POVERTY) and the HATE RATE for the 50 U.S. States and Washington, D.C.

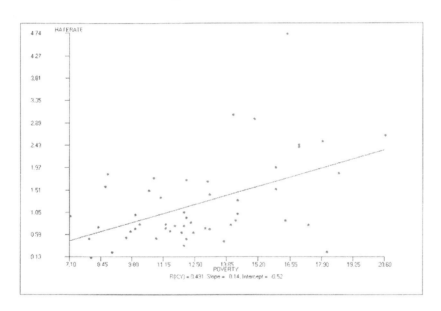

Note: The correlation coefficient, R[X,Y], of .491 is statistically significant at p = .000.

Finding: The higher the degree of income inequality, as measured by the Poverty Rate, the higher the HATE RATE.

Sources: The 2008/2009 HATE RATE data are from my Table 2, above. 2007 poverty rate data derive from the U.S. Census Bureau (2008).

Hypothesis 4: The higher the degree of existential insecurity within the United States, as measured by the Top 20% to Bottom 20% Income Ratio (TTPTBTPR), the higher the degree of manifest hate, as measured by my HATE RATE.

The results of the test of this hypothesis appear in Figure 4.

Figure 4: Relationship between the Top 20% to Bottom 20% Income Ratio (TTPTBTPR) and the HATE RATE for the 50 U.S. States and Washington, D.C.

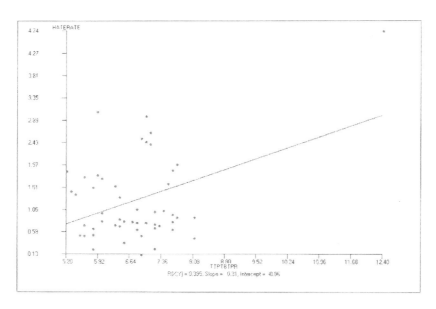

Note: The correlation coefficient, R[X,Y], of .395 is statistically significant at p = .004.

Finding: The higher the degree of income inequality, as measured by the Top 20% to Bottom 20% Income Ratio (TTPTBTPR), the higher the HATE RATE.

Sources: The 2008/2009 HATE RATE data are from my Table 2, above. 2007 Top 20% to Bottom 20% Income Ratio (TTPTBTPR) data derive from the U.S. Census Bureau (2008).

Existential Insecurity Resulting from Other Social Environment Stressors and their Effects on Manifest Hate

In addition to existential threats experienced as a result of individual and group positions of inequality within the economy, as measured by income inequalities, other areas of existential insecurity might reasonably be expected to show relationships with manifest hate as measured by my measure of manifest hate, the HATE RATE.

Existential Insecurity resulting from Low Levels of Educational Attainment and its Effect on Manifest Hate

Although in contemporary U.S. society, a college degree increases the likelihood of employment and the promise of substantially higher average lifetime income earnings, the basic credential for employment in living wage or even poverty level jobs remains the completion of high school.

Accordingly, our next hypothesis is:

Hypothesis 5: The higher the degree of existential insecurity within the United States, as measured by the High School Completion Rate (HSORMORE), the higher the degree of manifest hate, as measured by my HATE RATE.

The results of the test of this hypothesis appear in Figure 5.

Figure 5: Relationship between the High School Completion Rate (HSORMORE) and the HATE RATE for the 50 U.S. States and Washington, D.C.

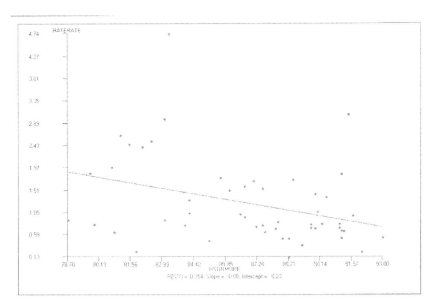

Note: The correlation coefficient, R[X,Y], of −.354 is statistically significant at p = .011.

Finding: The higher the degree of educational inequality, as measured by the High School Completion Rate (HSORMORE), the higher the HATE RATE. This finding may also be stated as follows: the lower the high school completion rate, the higher the HATE RATE, as portrayed by the upper right to lower left slope of the regression line

Sources: The 2008/2009 HATE RATE data are from my Table 2, above. 2007 educational attainment data derive from the U.S. Census Bureau (2008).

Existential Insecurity resulting from Membership in a Community of "Racial" or Ethnic Minority and its Effects on Manifest Hate

In contemporary United States society, African Americans and increasingly Hispanics, largely because of the Hispanics' real or perceived threatening rates of high immigration, have become targets of hate.

These realities justify the next two hypotheses.

Hypothesis 6: The higher the degree of existential insecurity within the United States, as measured by the percentages of African Americans (%BLACK), the higher the degree of manifest hate, as measured by my HATE RATE.

Figure 6: Relationship between the percentages of African Americans (%BLACK) and the HATE RATE for the 50 U.S. States and Washington, D.C.

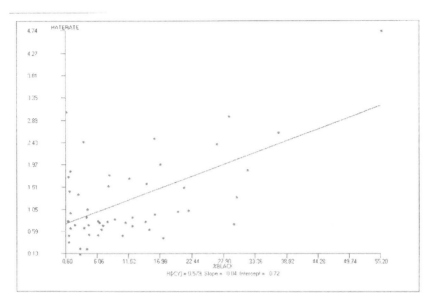

Note: The correlation coefficient, R[X,Y], of .579 is statistically significant at p = .000.

Finding: The higher the level of existential insecurity, as measured by the percentage of African Americans (%BLACK), the higher the HATE RATE.

Sources: The 2008/2009 HATE RATE data are from my Table 2, above. The percentages of African Americans in 2008 derive from *The 2008 Statistical Abstract of the United States*.

Hypothesis 7: The higher the degree of existential insecurity within the United States, as measured by the percentage growth of the Hispanic Population (%HISGRTH), the higher the degree of manifest hate, as measured by my HATE RATE.

Figure 7: Relationship between the percentage growth of the Hispanic Population (%HISGRTH) and the HATE RATE for the 50 U.S. States and Washington, D.C.

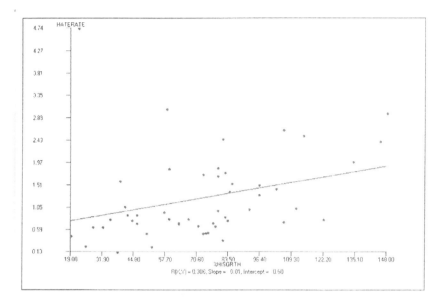

Note: The correlation coefficient, R[X,Y], of .306 is statistically significant at p = .029.

Finding: The higher the level of existential insecurity, as measured by the percentage growth of the Hispanic Population (%HISGRTH), the higher the HATE RATE.

Sources: The 2008/2009 HATE RATE data are from my Table 2, above. The percentage growth in the Hispanic Population data derive from *The 2010 Statistical Abstract of the United States.*

Existential Insecurity resulting from Gender Inequalities and their Effects on Manifest Hate

In recent years in the United States, average advances in education, employment and income of females *vis-à-vis* males may be a cause of male resentment, leading to probable increasing instances of manifest hate directed at females.

Therefore, the next hypothesis is:

Hypothesis 8: The higher the degree of existential insecurity within the United States, as measured by the Percentages of Females (%FEMALE), the higher the degree of manifest hate, as measured by my HATE RATE.

Figure 8: Relationship between the Percentages of Females (%FEMALE) and the HATE RATE for the 50 U.S. States and Washington, D.C.

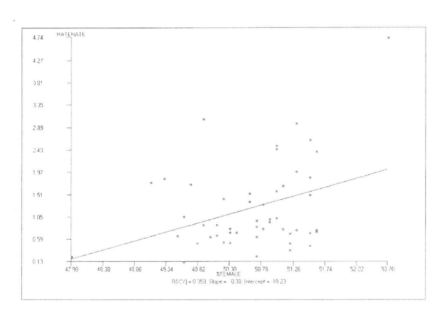

Note: The correlation coefficient, R[X,Y], of .359 is statistically significant at p = .010.

Finding: The higher the level of existential insecurity, as measured by the Percentages of Females (%FEMALE), the higher the HATE RATE.

Sources: The 2008/2009 HATE RATE data are from my Table 2, above. The 2008 percentages of female data derive from *The 2009 Statistical Abstract of the United States.*

Existential Insecurity related to Societal Health and Mortality and their Effects on Manifest Hate

The United States remains the only modern industrial society that does not provide guaranteed universal health care to its citizenry.

For millions of Americans, lack of access to affordable health care is likely a chronic source of existential threat.

There are numerous measures or indicators of societal health and mortality, including, the obesity rate, the smoking rate, the teen pregnancy rate, the teen birth rate, the overall health of a state's population, the well-being of a state's population, the state infant mortality rate, the life expectancy of a state's population, and the state's score on the Human Development Index.

The probable effects of each of these measures of societal health are considered in the hypotheses and associated findings that follow.

Hypothesis 9: The higher the degree of existential insecurity within the United States, as measured by the Adult Obesity Rate (OBESITY), the higher the degree of manifest hate, as measured by my HATE RATE.

Figure 9: Relationship between the Adult Obesity Rate (OBESITY), and the HATE RATE for the 50 U.S. States and Washington, D.C.

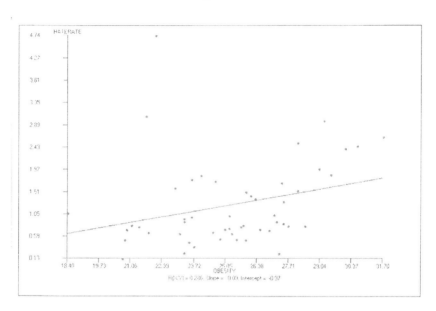

Note: The correlation coefficient, R[X,Y], of .286 is statistically significant at p = .042.

Finding: The higher the level of existential insecurity, as measured by the Obesity Rate (OBESITY), the higher the HATE RATE.

Sources: The 2008/2009 HATE RATE data are from my Table 2, above. The 2009 "Adult Obesity Rates, percent of obese adults (those with a 2007-2009 Body Mass Index [BM] average of 30.0 to 99.8) for the 50 U.S. states and Washington, D.C.," derive from the National Center for Chronic Disease and Health Promotion of the Centers for Disease Control (2009).

Hypothesis 10: The higher the degree of existential insecurity within the United States, as measured by the Adult Smoking Rate

(SMOKRATE), the higher the degree of manifest hate, as measured by my HATE RATE.

Figure 10: Relationship between the Adult Smoking Rate (SMOKRATE), and the HATE RATE for the 50 U.S. States and Washington, D.C.

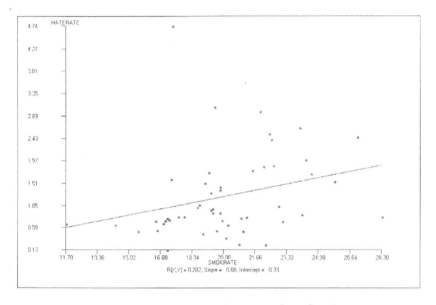

Note: The correlation coefficient, R[X,Y], of .282 is statistically significant at p = .045.

Finding: The higher the level of existential insecurity, as measured by the Adult Smoking Rate (SMOKRATE), the higher the HATE RATE.

Sources: The 2008/2009 HATE RATE data are from my Table 2, above. The percentage of state adult populations smoking cigarettes for the year 2008 derive from the Behavioral Risk Factor Surveillance System of the Centers for Disease Control (2009).

Hypothesis 11: The higher the degree of existential insecurity within the United States, as measured by the Teen (Ages 15 – 19) Pregnancy

Rate (PREGRATE), the higher the degree of manifest hate, as measured by my HATE RATE.

Figure 11: Relationship between the Teen (Ages 15 – 19) Pregnancy Rate (PREGRATE) and the HATE RATE for the 50 U.S. States and Washington, D.C.

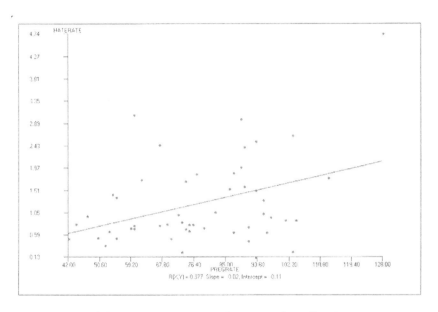

Note: The correlation coefficient, R[X,Y], of .377 is statistically significant at p = .006.

Finding: The higher the level of existential insecurity, as measured by the Teen (Ages 15 – 19) Pregnancy Rate (PREGRATE), the higher the HATE RATE.

Sources: The 2008/2009 HATE RATE data are from my Table 2, above. The 2000 teen pregnancy rates derive from the Guttmacher Institute "Rates of pregnancy … among women aged 15-19, by age group, according to state of residence" (2010).

Hypothesis 12: The higher the degree of existential insecurity within the United States, as measured by the Teen (Ages 15 – 19) Birth Rate

(BIRTHS), the higher the degree of manifest hate, as measured by my HATE RATE.

Figure 12: Relationship between the Teen (Ages 15 – 19) Birth Rate (BIRTHS) and the HATE RATE for the 50 U.S. States and Washington, D.C.

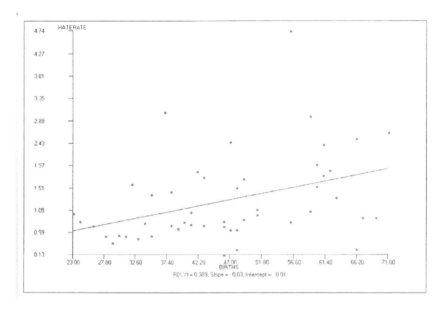

Note: The correlation coefficient, R[X,Y], of .389 is statistically significant at p = .005.

Finding: The higher the level of existential insecurity, as measured by the Teen (Ages 15 – 19) Birth Rate (BIRTHS), the higher the HATE RATE.

Sources: The 2008/2009 HATE RATE data are from my Table 2, above. The 2000 teen birth rates derive from the Guttmacher Institute "Rates of ... birth ... among women aged 15-19, by age group, according to state of residence" (2010).

Hypothesis 13: The higher the degree of existential insecurity within the United States, as measured by a state's Overall Health (HEALTH), the higher the degree of manifest hate, as measured by my HATE RATE.

Figure 13: Relationship between a state's Overall Health (HEALTH) and the HATE RATE for the 50 U.S. States. Data were unavailable for Washington, D.C.

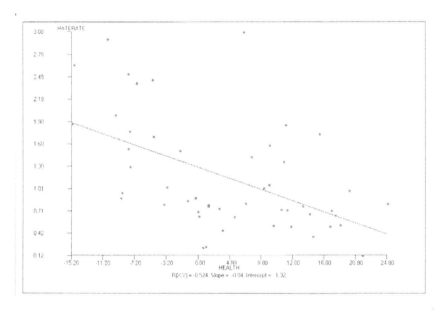

Note: The correlation coefficient, R[X,Y], of − .524 is statistically significant at p = .000.

Finding: The higher the level of existential insecurity, as measured by a state's Overall Health (HEALTH), the higher the HATE RATE. This finding may also be stated as follows: The lower the level of a state's overall health, the higher the hate rate. Once again, the slope of the regression line from upper left to lower right graphically portrays this reality.

Sources: The 2008/2009 HATE RATE data are from my Table 2, above. The "Overall Health" composite variable includes a variety of measures of state health in 2007 and incorporates them into a combined indicator …

The core measures comprising the composite include such "Behaviors" as prevalence of obesity, smoking, and binge drinking; "Community and Environment" factors, such as occupational fatalities per 100,000 workers, infectious disease per 100,000 population, air pollution ("micrograms of fine particles per cubic meter"), and percent of children in poverty; "Public and Health Policies," focused on percent of the population without health insurance, immunization coverage, and public health funding; "Clinical Care," such as prenatal care, preventable hospitalization, and number of primary care physicians per 100,000 population; and the "Health Outcomes" of premature death ("years lost per 100,000 population"), poor physical health days ("in the previous 30 days"), infant mortality, poor mental health days, cancer deaths, and cardiovascular deaths, each calculated per 100,000 population.

The measure of a state's overall health derives from the work of the United Health Foundation (2009).

Hypothesis 14: The higher the degree of existential insecurity within the United States, as measured by the Well-Being Index (WELLBEIN), the higher the degree of manifest hate, as measured by my HATE RATE.

Figure 14: Relationship between the Well-Being Index (WELLBEIN) and the HATE RATE for the 50 U.S. States. Data were unavailable for Washington, D.C.

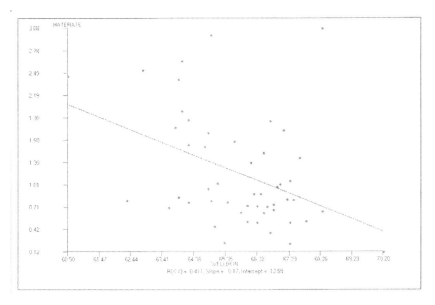

Note: The correlation coefficient, R[X,Y], of − .411 is statistically significant at p = .003.

Finding: The higher the level of existential insecurity, as measured by a state's Well-Being (WELLBEIN), the higher the HATE RATE. This finding may also be stated as follows: The lower the level of a state's well-being, the higher the hate rate.

Sources: The 2008/2009 HATE RATE data are from my Table 2, above. The Gallup-Healthways Well-Being Index is the first-ever daily assessment of U.S. residents' health and well-being. "By interviewing at least 1,000 U.S. adults every day, the Well-Being Index provides real-time measurement and insights needed to improve health, increase productivity, and lower healthcare costs. Public and private sector leaders use data on life evaluation, physical health, emotional health, healthy behavior, work environment, and basic access to develop and prioritize strategies to help their communities thrive and grow. Journalists, academics, and medical experts benefit from this unprecedented resource of health statistics and behavioral economic data to inform their research and reporting." The Gallup-Healthways Well-Being Index values for 2008 are available online.

Hypothesis 15: The higher the degree of existential insecurity within the United States, as measured by the Infant Mortality Rate (INFANMOR), the higher the degree of manifest hate, as measured by my HATE RATE.

Figure 15: Relationship between the Infant Mortality Rate (INFANMOR) and the HATE RATE for the 50 U.S. States and Washington, D.C.

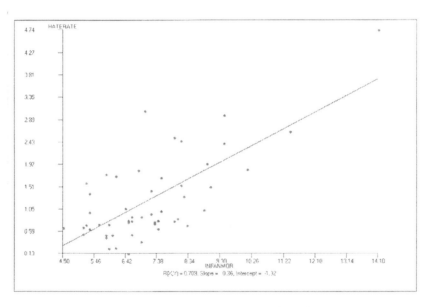

Note: The correlation coefficient, R[X,Y], of .709 is statistically significant at p = .000.

Finding: The higher the level of existential insecurity, as measured by Infant Mortality Rate (INFANMOR), the higher the HATE RATE.

Sources: The 2008/2009 HATE RATE data are from my Table 2, above. The "Number of infant deaths (aged 0-1 year) per 1,000 live births for the year 2005" derive from the Centers for Disease Control and Prevention (2006).

Hypothesis 16: The higher the degree of existential insecurity within the United States, as measured by the Life Expectancy (LIFEXEP), the higher the degree of manifest hate, as measured by my HATE RATE.

Figure 16: Relationship between the Life Expectancy (LIFEXEP) and the HATE RATE for the 50 U.S. States and Washington, D.C.

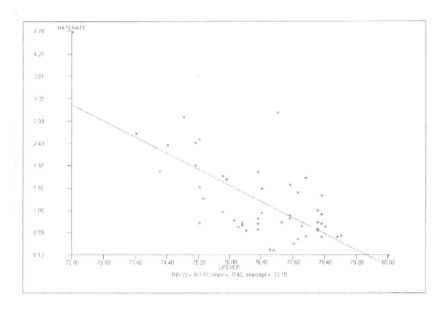

Note: The correlation coefficient, R[X,Y], of − .720 is statistically significant at p = .000.

Finding: The higher the level of existential insecurity, as measured by the Life Expectancy (LIFEXEP), the higher the HATE RATE. This finding may also be stated as follows: The lower the Life Expectancy, the higher the level of manifest hate. Again, the upper left to lower right slope of the regression line portrays this finding graphically.

Sources: The 2008/2009 HATE RATE data are from my Table 2, above. The "Average life expectancies from birth" data derive from the Harvard University School of Public Health (2009).

Hypothesis 17: The higher the degree of existential insecurity within the United States, as measured by the Human Development Index (HDI), the higher the degree of manifest hate, as measured by my HATE RATE.

Figure 17: Relationship between the Human Development Index (HDI) and the HATE RATE for the 50 U.S. States and Washington, D.C.

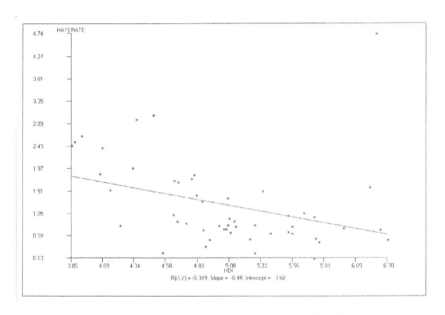

Note: The correlation coefficient, R[X,Y], of − .349 is statistically significant at p = .012.

Finding: The higher the level of existential insecurity, as measured by the Human Development Index (HDI), the higher the HATE RATE. This finding may also be stated as follows: The lower the score on the Human Development Index, the higher the level of manifest hate

Sources: The 2008/2009 HATE RATE data are from my Table 2, above. The Human Development Index (HDI) is a composite indicator of national growth or development that has been used since 1990 by the United Nations as a people-focused alternative to traditional economic indicators (such as the GNP and GDP) and that includes educational attainment, average life expectancy, and median household income.

An initiative of the Social Science Research Council (SSRC), the "American Human Development Project" designed *The Modified American Human Development Index*, with scores for the 50 U.S. States and Washington, D.C., ranging from 6.30 for Connecticut to 3.85 for West Virginia. The HDI data derive from the Social Science Research Council (2010).

Existential Insecurity related to Crime and Punishment and its Effects on Manifest Hate

If it is reasonable to argue that high rates of crime and prison incarceration may be indicative of and/or contribute to feelings of existential insecurity and be related directly or indirectly to manifest hate, then the following three hypotheses appear warranted:

Hypothesis 18: The higher the degree of existential insecurity within the United States, as measured by the Violent Crime Rate (VICRATE), the higher the degree of manifest hate, as measured by my HATE RATE.

Figure 18: Relationship between the Violent Crime Rate (VICRATE) and the HATE RATE for the 50 U.S. States and Washington, D.C.

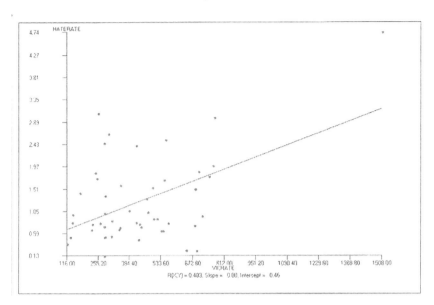

Note: The correlation coefficient, R[X,Y], of .483 is statistically significant at p = .000.

Finding: The higher the level of existential insecurity, as measured by the Violent Crime Rate (VICRATE), the higher the HATE RATE.

Sources: The 2008/2009 HATE RATE data are from my Table 2, above. Data on "Violent crimes per 100,000 population" derive from the U.S. Department of Justice, Federal Bureau of Investigation (2006).

Hypothesis 19: The higher the degree of existential insecurity within the United States, as measured by the Murder Rate (MURRATE), the higher the degree of manifest hate, as measured by my HATE RATE.

Figure 19: Relationship between the Murder Rate (MURRATE) and the HATE RATE for the 50 U.S. States and Washington, D.C.

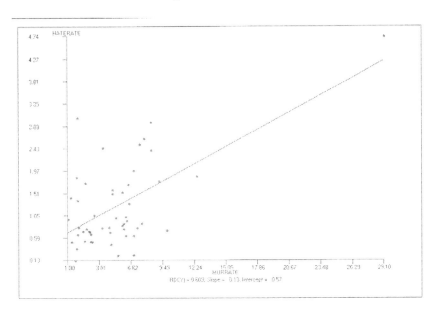

Note: The correlation coefficient, R[X,Y], of .609 is statistically significant at p = .000.

Finding: The higher the level of existential insecurity, as measured by the Murder Rate (MURRATE), the higher the HATE RATE. Look at where Washington, D.C.s, dot appears at the upper far right of the scatter diagram. It is the city of Disgraceful Contrasts, indeed.

Sources: The 2008/2009 HATE RATE data are from my Table 2, above. Data on "Homicides (including negligent manslaughter) per 100,000 population" derive from the U.S. Department of Justice, Federal Bureau of Investigation (2006).

Hypothesis 20: The higher the degree of existential insecurity within the United States, as measured by the Prison Incarceration Rate

(INCARATE), the higher the degree of manifest hate, as measured by my HATE RATE.

Figure 20: Relationship between the Prison Incarceration Rate (INCARATE) and the HATE RATE for the 50 U.S. States and Washington, D.C.

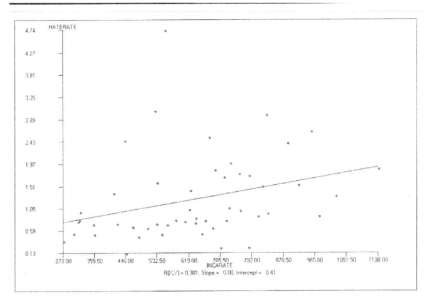

Note: The correlation coefficient, R[X,Y], of .301 is statistically significant at p = .032.

Finding: The higher the level of existential insecurity, as measured by the Prison Incarceration Rate (INCARATE), the higher the HATE RATE.

Sources: The 2008/2009 HATE RATE data are from my Table 12, above. The "Inmates per 100,000 residents at mid-year, 2005" data derive from the Bureau of Justice Statistics (2008).

Existential Insecurity related to Extreme Religiosity and its Effects on Manifest Hate

There is an old admonition that can be found in many societies and cultures, both ancient and modern, that encourages "moderation in all things."

It is certainly the case that too much of even a good thing can be bad for your health and well-being, even practicing such otherwise exemplary virtues as hard work, exercise, high fiber diets, and generosity toward others of your attention, time, and money.

According to my own research on religion and religiosity, as well as the research and theorizing of several others, too much faith, whether expressed as beliefs, attitudes, or behaviors, can have negative consequences, and actually even be indicative of a kind of social problem or instance of societal dysfunction.

Attempting to reconcile alternative explanations for religiosity and religious behavior developed by proponents and opponents of the "secularization hypothesis," for example, Pippa Norris and Ronald Inglehart in their 2004 ground-breaking book, *Sacred and Secular*, sought a middle-ground or synthesis by invoking the concept of *societal and personal insecurity* (existential insecurity), the concept that figures prominently in my own current and ongoing research (2004: 3-32):

> There is no question that the traditional secularization thesis needs updating. It is obvious that religion has not disappeared from the world, nor does it seem likely to do so. Nevertheless, the concept of secularization captures an important part of what is going on …

> This book *Sacred and Secular* develops a revised version of secularization theory that emphasizes the extent to which people have a sense of *existential security* – that is,

the feeling that survival is secure enough that it can be taken for granted …

We believe that the importance of religiosity persists most strongly among vulnerable populations, especially those living in poorer nations, facing personal survival-threatening risks …

We argue that feelings of vulnerability to physical, societal, and personal risks are a key factor driving religiosity and we demonstrate that the process of secularization – a systematic erosion of religious practices, values, and beliefs – has occurred most clearly among the most prosperous social sectors living in affluent and secure post-industrial nations (2004, pp. 4-5).

Religiosity Data for my Research on Existential Insecurity Resulting from Extreme Religiosity and its Effects on Manifest Hate

The Pew Forum on Religion and Public Life 2008 *U.S. Religious Landscape Survey*, the results of which were published in 2009 and which involved a representative probability sample of over 35,000 adults, contained a series of questions pertaining to religious beliefs and practices.

My original and novel composite measure or indicator of *extreme religiosity* derives from the states' percentage shares of survey respondents answering as follows to five select religious beliefs and practices question: (a) they are *"absolutely certain* that God exists;" (b) they "believe the *Bible* to be the *actual word of God*, literally true, word for word;" (c) they assert that "religion is a *very important* part of their daily lives;" (d) they "attend religious services *at least once a week*;" and (e) they "pray *at least once a day*."

In addition to asking survey respondents about their religious beliefs and practices, questions were asked about denominational affiliation.

Of the entire sample, 84% identified with one of the following "major religious traditions:" Evangelical Protestant (26%); Mainline Protestant (18%); Catholic (24%); and Unaffiliated (16%). No tradition other than these exceeded 10%.

The next largest group self-identified with Historically Black Churches at 7%, with the Jewish tradition at only 1.7%; Buddhists comprised but .7% and Muslims and Hindus were .6% and .4%, respectively. Among the Unaffiliated were Atheists at 1.6%, Agnostics at 2.4% and "Nothing in particular" at 12.1%.

Of the major religious traditions, Evangelical Protestants are clearly the most "extreme," in general, regarding their commitments to proselytizing and attempting to influence positions on economic, political, and social issues, such as those involving separation of church and state, abortion, homosexual marriage, progressive taxation of income and wealth, redistribution of wealth, and the like.

The above religiosity data allow us to test two hypotheses.

Hypothesis 21: The higher the degree of existential insecurity within the United States, as measured by my measure of Extreme Religiosity of Beliefs and Practices (HIGHREL), the higher the degree of manifest hate, as measured by my HATE RATE.

Figure 21: Relationship between my measure of Extreme Religiosity of Beliefs and Practices (HIGHREL) and the HATE RATE for 50 U.S. States and Washington, D.C.

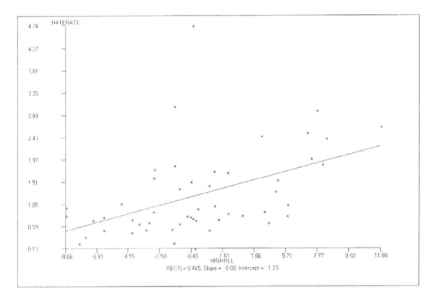

Note: The correlation coefficient, R[X,Y], of .465 is statistically significant at p = .001.

Finding: The higher the level of existential insecurity, as measured by Extreme Religiosity (HIGHREL), the higher the HATE RATE.

Sources: The 2008/2009 HATE RATE data are from my Table 2, above. The Extreme Religiosity of Beliefs and Practices measure data derive from the Pew Forum on Religion and Public Life *U.S. Religious Landscape Survey* (2009). This figure appears also in an article I wrote and published in 2012 under my French pseudonym, R. Georges Delamontagne. It is "Relationships between Varieties of Religious Experience and Manifest Hate: A Sociological Analysis." *Journal of Religion and Society* 14: 1-25.

Hypothesis 22: The higher the degree of existential insecurity within the United States, as measured by Self-Identification with the Evangelical Protestant Tradition (EVANPROT), the higher the degree of manifest hate, as measured by my HATE RATE.

Figure 22: Relationship between Self-Identification with the Evangelical Protestant Tradition (EVANPROT) and the HATE RATE for 50 U.S. States and Washington, D.C.

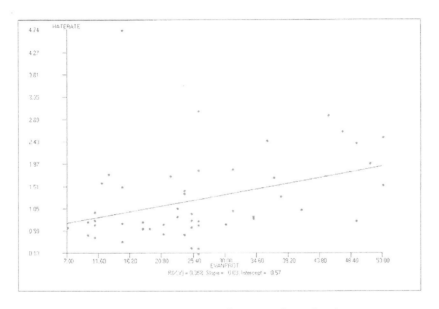

Note: The correlation coefficient, $R[X,Y]$, of .358 is statistically significant at $p = .010$.

Finding: The higher the level of existential insecurity, as measured by Self-Identification with the Evangelical Protestant Tradition (EVANPROT), the higher the HATE RATE.

Sources: The 2008/2009 HATE RATE data are from my Table 2, above. The Self-Identification with the Evangelical Protestant Tradition data derive from the Pew Forum on Religion and Public Life *U.S.*

Religious Landscape Survey (2009). This figure appears also the article I cited among the sources in Figure 21.

A Concluding Note on 'Moderation in All Things'

From our tests of our last two hypotheses, we discovered that even extremes of religiosity can have negative or undesirable consequences.

In that regard, I feel certain that you will not be surprised to learn that, based upon my own related research, that moderation of religious beliefs and practices, as measured by my Pew Forum Religion and Public Life *U.S. Religious Landscape Survey* data, displayed a negative relationship with manifest hate, as measured by my HATE RATE: The higher the percentage of religious moderates, the lower the HATE RATE.

See the article I wrote and published in 2012 under my French pseudonym, R. Georges Delamontagne. It is cited as a source in both Figure 21 and Figure 22.

Similarly, I found through my research that the Percentage of Mainline Protestants, as opposed to Evangelical Protestants, is absolutely unrelated to the HATE RATE; namely, it does not affect it, either negatively or positively.

Finally, I found that the Percentage of Catholics, is negatively to the HATE RATE; namely, the higher the Percentage of Catholics, the lower the HATE RATE.

Does Catholicism promote love more than hate? The answer would appear to be in the affirmative, based upon my research findings.

Once again, this finding is reported in the article I wrote and published in 2012 under my French pseudonym, R. Georges Delamontagne, "Relationships between Varieties of Religious Experience and Manifest Hate: A Sociological Analysis." *Journal of Religion and Society* 14: 1-25.

Summary of Our Research Findings Regarding the Effects of Existential Insecurity Resulting from a Wide Variety of Social Environment Stressors on Manifest Hate

In the preceding pages of this chapter, we presented evidence demonstrating that when testing hypotheses focusing on 22 measures or indicators of existential insecurity, and their relationships to manifest hate, we displayed findings demonstrating the confirmation or support of each and every one of the hypotheses.

Whether measured by the economic inequality existential insecurity stressors of the Gini Coefficient, the Median Household Income, the Poverty Rate, or the Top 20% to Bottom 20% Income Ratio, we found consistently, and without exception, that, the higher the level of existential insecurity deriving from economic inequality, the higher the level of manifest hate, as measured by my HATE RATE.

Similarly, we found that low levels of educational attainment, high percentages of racial or ethnic minorities, and high percentage of females, since racial and ethnic minorities, as well as females have become increasingly important victims of manifest hate, correlated, in predicted ways, with manifest hate, as measured by my HATE RATE.

We found also that a wide variety of measures societal health and mortality, including the adult obesity rate, the adult smoking rate, the teen pregnancy rate, the teen birth rate, the infant mortality rate, the life expectancy rate, and the state score on the Human Development Index (HDI) related in predicted ways with my measure of manifest hate, the HATE RATE.

Our examination of the relationships between our measures of the violent crime rate, the murder rate, and the prison incarceration rate with the HATE RATE showed that crime and prison incarceration correlate, again in predicted ways, with manifest hate. The higher the violent crime rate, the higher the murder rate, and the higher the prison incarceration rate, the higher the HATE RATE.

Finally, we found that the old adage of "moderation in all things" applies to religious beliefs and practices as well as denominational affiliation.

Before leaving this chapter and moving on to the last part and concluding chapter of this book, it is most important that we consider and discuss the very real and most embarrassing reality that is our Washington, D.C., the capital of our United States of America. It's sad, but true. Woe is us.

A Note on a Recurring Statistical Outlier, the Disturbing Case of Washington, D.C.

As I explained, based on common sense and the findings of down-to-earth sociological research reported in my recent book, *Economic Inequality and What YOU Can Do About It: A Primer and Call to Action!*:

> The capital of the United States, Washington, D.C. is an extraordinary exemplar of social problems, societal mal-adaptation and dysfunction, and I have recently decided that an appropriate moniker is for it to be designated as the city of 'Disgraceful Contrasts.' Surrounded contiguously by some of the nation's wealthiest upper-class and upper-middle class neighborhoods of Georgetown, the rest of Northwest Washington, Bethesda, Chevy Chase, Potomac and McLean, Virginia, as this reality has been recently described graphically, dramatically, and convincingly by Charles Murray in his *Coming Apart: The State of White America, 1960 – 2010* (2012), not only does Washington, D.C., have the highest levels of income inequality as measured by the Gini Coefficient, it also has the nation's highest child poverty rate; the highest top 20% to bottom 20% income ratio; the highest teen pregnancy and abortion rates; the highest infant mortality rate; the lowest average life expectancy; and the highest violent crime and murder rates.

> It is no wonder that such a nexus of social pathology is also home to the largest proportional representation of active hate groups. The ratio of the Washington, D.C., percentage share of active hate groups to its percentage share of the United States' population is 4.74, meaning, of course, that it had 3.74 times more active hate groups

than would be expected on the basis of its population size.

Several of these hate groups may very well have located
in D.C. largely because it is the nation's capital, a major
center of both concentrated political power and high
levels of income and wealth inequality....

It is also not surprising that Arianna Huffington, author
of *Third World America*, has referred to Washington,
D.C., as "A Third World Capital" (2010).

Yes, I know that I am repeating myself by, once again, quoting
Arianna Huffington, but it's a reality worth repeating because of its
seriousness and what it says about our national economic, political and
social priorities. Disgraceful Contrasts, indeed.

If you look carefully at my above hypotheses and research findings concerning the relationships between all of the 22 measures of
existential insecurity and manifest hate, as measured by my HATE
RATE, you will observe that our nation's capital, Washington, D.C.,
is Distinguished Curiously by its extraordinarily high level of manifest
hate, namely, the HATE RATE, of 4.735 (or, rounded to the next
number, 4.74), the absolute highest in the nation. Shameful, for sure.

The next three highest HATE RATES are to be found in Montana
at 3.075, South Carolina at 2.99, and Mississippi at 2.65. See my Tables
1 and 2 above.

States displaying the lowest levels of manifest hate include my
home state of Maine, with its HATE RATE of .38, as well as New
Mexico at .25, Alaska at .235, and Hawaii at .125.

Incidentally, my wife Nancy and I chose quite deliberately to
retire in Greenville, South Carolina, a city of delightfully open-minded,
diverse, and tolerant people. We love living in Greenville! In most cities
throughout the United States, haters are in the minority, fortunately.

While the State Hate Index (SHI) value for South Carolina is
substantially greater than it is for Maine, there are many, many people in

both states who readily join you and me in our commitments to respect diversity, teach tolerance, and fight hate. Lucky us.

PART III

What You and I Can do to Combat
and Reduce Manifest Hate

Chapter 6
Respect Diversity – Teach Tolerance – Fight Hate!

Before we can fruitfully discuss ways in which we might most effectively work together to help reduce levels of manifest hate, it is important to remind ourselves of how deeply hate is rooted in human nature. It is a component of our biological, our psychological, and our social selves.

Recall from earlier chapters that hate is a secondary emotion deriving from the primary emotions of fear, anger, and disgust. Recall further that fear and anger are triggered by the fight or flight response of our autonomic nervous system, and that those responses have deep roots in our evolutionary history as a species.

Since hate is grounded in human emotion, it becomes especially challenging to restrain, control, or minimize it. Our greatest weapons in this never-ending battle are truth, reason, and appeals to compassion.

Recall also from our discussion of the psychology of hate that the Sternbergs' Duplex Theory of Hate provided a useful framework for describing and analyzing hate.

For the Sternbergs, hate is most usefully described and analyzed metaphorically (not strictly geometrically) in terms of the vertices of a *triangle* or triangles involving three components; namely, Negation of Intimacy (-I) (comprised of the primary emotion of *disgust*), Passion (P) (based upon the primary emotions of *anger/fear*), and Commitment

(C) (devaluation/ diminution), reflecting the human cognitive or mental states, as opposed to the strictly emotional components of hate.

As previously emphasized by the Sternbergs, hate triangles, taken by themselves, are insufficient for a complete duplex theory of hate, for their very existence is dependent upon accompanying stories, which function to describe the real or imagined characteristics of the target of hate, usually as compared with the perpetrator(s) of hate.

These stories, as you and I have previously observed, exist in our society and culture.

In the Sternberg duplex theory of hate, a typology of common stories of hate was developed, whereby the categories of stories were described in terms of their hypothesized relationships to the triangular components of Negation of Intimacy (-I), Passion (P), and Commitment (C).

Recall our earlier mention of some of the common stories, such as "stranger (vs. in-group)," "impure other (vs. pure in-group)," "enemy of God (vs. servant of God)," "controller (vs. controlled)," "barbarian (vs. civilized in group)," "greedy enemy (vs. financially responsible in-group)," "criminal (vs. innocent party)," "animal pest (vs. human)," and "comic character (vs. sensible in-group)," to identify but a few of these possible stories.

The biological, psychological, and sociological realities of hate that we have just discussed provide a useful framework for our efforts to respect diversity, teach tolerance, and fight hate.

There are at least four things we can do to advance our agenda: (1st) live our daily lives in ways that display our commitments to our values; (2nd) join with others in organized efforts to promote respect for diversity, teach tolerance, and fight hate; (3rd) become active in and support existing groups and organizations, local, state, and national, that share our values; and (4th), last but not least, fight those 'existential stressors' in our social environments that are likely to trigger the feelings of 'existential insecurity' that are so closely related to hate.

Living Exemplary Lives

Living exemplary lives dedicated to respect for diversity and tolerance for those who are different should be easy for most Americans. After all, the first sentence of the second paragraph of the July 4, 1776, document we refer to as *The Declaration of Independence* reads "We hold these truths to be self-evident, that all men are created equal, that they are endowed by their Creator with certain unalienable Rights, that among these are Life, Liberty and the pursuit of Happiness."

Of course, those who wrote these words were white men, who were owners of property, 'property' that included other men and women, mostly black, slaves.

While the white propertied men did not consider their wives to be slaves, most of them probably treated them as being somehow less equal then they were; namely, the men were likely, in substantial numbers, misogynists, at least to some degree.

Similarly, several amendments to the *United States Constitution* also provided both moral and legal foundations for our embracing and living lives based upon ideals of equality and diversity.

While we tend to take the amendments today, like the words of *The Declaration of Independence*, as self-evident truths, they were, in fact, quite revolutionary in human history, and hard battles had to be fought by determined progressive forces to attain the rights that the amendments conferred upon U.S. citizens.

Five of the twenty-seven amendments that are most directly relevant to the purposes of this book are the: 1st, enacted in 1791, that established freedom of speech, freedom of religion, freedom of the press, and the right to assemble and petition the government; 13th, enacted in 1865, that abolished slavery; 15th, enacted in 1870, that prohibited the denial of suffrage based on race, color, or previous condition of servitude; 19th, enacted in 1920, that established women's suffrage; and 24th, enacted in 1964, that prohibited the revocation of voting rights due to the non-payment of poll taxes.

Much like we owe the authors of both *The Declaration of Independence* and our *United States Constitution* and its several amendments a debt of gratitude for their contributions to our progress as a nation, so too did our founding fathers ride on the shoulders of the giants who preceded them, or, in some cases, wrote along with them.

I am referring here, of course, primarily to the philosophers of the Eighteenth-Century, a time that came to be known as *The Age of Enlightenment* or *The Age of Reason*, a period in the history of human-kind that "shook the foundations of Western civilization," and that championed such "radical ideas as individual liberty."

Enlightenment philosophers wrote about such revolutionary topics as progress, tolerance, free-thinking, reason, common sense, equality and inequality, political justice, economic liberty, war and peace, slavery in America, and many more ground-breaking and *status quo* threatening notions.

Among the most frequently quoted and influential of the writers of the enlightenment were several notable names, at least some of which you will undoubtedly immediately recognize, such as Immanuel Kant, Francis Bacon, Isaac Newton, Benjamin Franklin, John Locke, Jean-Jacques Rousseau, Thomas Jefferson, Thomas Paine, James Madison, Jeremy Bentham, William Godwin, David Hume, Adam Smith, Denis Diderot, and Voltaire.

As you can see, our ideas of respect for diversity, teaching tolerance, and fighting hate, did not just drop out of the blue sky or pop into your and my heads.

People have been thinking about these ideas and ideals for a very long time. Lucky us.

We have, therefore, a firm foundation in enlightened and progressive thought to feel very good about living our exemplary lives, lives emphasizing our core values of respect for diversity, tolerance, and equality.

Since you already know how to and are already living those lives, and of this, I have no doubt, I have nothing more to advise you to do in that regard, except to cheer you on and encourage you to continue doing what you do every day.

Think of me as your number one fan club member and exuberant cheerleader.

There is one sense, however, in which all of us can do a much, much better, more active, and more aggressive job in attaining our mutually shared enlightenment and founding-father ideals.

We have to confront, head-on, disrespect of diversity, intolerance, and manifest hate, wherever and whenever they rear their ugly little heads in our day-to-day lives!

Confronting Disrespect of Diversity, Intolerance, and Manifest Hate in Our Daily Lives

As noble, important, and self-satisfying as it is to live exemplary lives of respect for diversity, teaching tolerance, and fighting hate we must oppose their enemies, at each and every opportunity.

It won't be easy. Recall that hate is, first and foremost, grounded in the primary human emotions of "fear and anger," Sternbergs' Passion (P), "disgust" or Negation of Intimacy (-I), and also in the cognitive or mental component of Commitment (C), involving "devaluation/ diminution."

This hard three-layered nut, in both the figurative and literal meanings of 'nut,' is a tough one crack. But, with the sharp and squirrely teeth of truth, reason, appeals to compassion, and downright tenacity, we can crack the unsavory nut.

Lacking squirrely teeth, we can buy those fabricated metal lobster-shell-cracking devices that are so popular in my home state of Maine.

By tooth or by fabricated metal device, we must combat hate and its antecedents and concomitants of fear, anger, and disgust, at every opportunity.

Every once in a while, such an opportunity presents itself, and, for one reason or another, we miss it, only later to regret it and reflect upon "What I should have said or done was …." But, the sad reality is that those missed opportunities normally can never be reclaimed.

About ten or so years ago, my wife, Nancy, and I were having dinner with s group of people, including both friends and strangers, in a summer month in my home state of Maine.

For those of you who don't know much about Maine, it is, on balance, a relatively independent state, as states go. Maine has historically had Democratic, Republican, and Independent Governors, and, in recent history, both Democratic and Republican majorities in both the State House and Senate.

In any event, at that dinner table of missed opportunity, for which Nancy and I will never, ever forgive ourselves, one of the people at the table, in the course of a discussion of a topic that I can no longer even recall, stated, ever-so-matter-of-factly and nonchalantly, that "In the South, we call it 'Nigger-rigged,'" presumably referring to a job of some sort that was not well-done, but rather completed, or not completed, in a sloppy, haphazard, or ineffective way.

So surprised and dumbfounded were we by this totally off-the wall and unexpected remark, in Maine at least, that our jaws dropped, so-to-speak, leaving us speechless, and it was not until after we had left the dinner that we spoke about it.

Incidentally, while the person at the dinner table did, in fact, reside in the South, at least during the winter months, I do not mean to suggest that all Southerners are racist haters and that all Northerners are not. As my data on hate groups have shown, hate groups and haters can be found in all or most states.

Although my home state is Maine, Nancy is a native of South Carolina. We chose to retire in Greenville, South Carolina, which is a wonderfully diverse and cosmopolitan city of friendly, generous, welcoming, and tolerant people, representing racial, ethnic, language, age, and other, diversity. All you have to do is visit Greenville's vibrant downtown to experience first-hand what I am talking about. It's a great place to live.

Similarly, most Americans, regardless of where they live, are not haters. Racists and bigots are, fortunately, among the minority in most places.

Regarding the incident at the dinner table that summer night in Maine, the truth is that we have never forgiven ourselves about not taking that opportunity to set the record straight.

What we should have said was something along the lines of "We're sorry to interrupt, but we find your use of the expression 'Nigger-rigged' as most offensive and unacceptable, and we respectfully demand that you retract and repudiate it."

We could and should have gone on to state that "Such an assertion is unbecoming a supposedly educated and compassionate human being."

"Furthermore, if you really think about it, the thing that frustrates you is sloppy work, and that is what the focus of your frustration or anger should be directed toward. Not against someone whose skin color happens to be, by birth, different than yours."

All of us, whether we are white, black, yellow, or red, or any and all shades among and between; male or female; gay, lesbian, bisexual, transgendered, or straight; American, South African, Italian, Yugoslav, French, German, or Dutch, are capable of sloppy work.

Hate the sloppy work, not the social group or social category to which the person who does the sloppy work belongs.

Needless to say, had we interjected either or both of those statements in the conversation at the dinner table, we would have both affected the appetites of those at the dinner table, and probably given indigestion to some, sullied our otherwise jovial and friendly personas, and be denied any future dinner invitations.

The point is that we would have readily and willingly been ready to bear the consequences, but we were so totally surprised and caught flat-footed, by the remark on "Nigger-rigged," that we missed the opportunity to do the right thing.

Although there are no easy, ready-made, and off-the-shelf recipes for combating disrespect for diversity, intolerance, and manifest hate, reminding ourselves that they are grounded in the primal human emotions of fear, anger, and disgust, and that they are triggered by stories, however false and insidious, commonly found in the general culture, and especially in the subcultures of intolerance and hate, we have to be ever-persistent, like the Energizer Bunny, to keep on going, going, and going.

The best chance we have for changing hateful habits of the heart and brain, are by appeals to facts, logic, reason, and compassion. If those don't work, don't feel guilty by relying on efforts to shame the haters. They, after all, deserve it.

Since many haters are also extremely religious in a blind, unreflective, and frequently distorted way, and as I have described in my own sociological research, presented in Chapter 6, especially in the last two figures of that chapter, it might be helpful to try to appeal to the better part of their religious selves.

Remind them that Jesus Christ preached the gospel of love, not hate, and also of the Golden Rule, "Do Unto Others as You Would Have Them Do Unto You." Also, gently, but persuasively, ply them with facts and supportive evidence that their eyes and ears cannot readily deny.

Finally, if all else fails, call them out for what they are, absolute disgraces to their supposed religious beliefs.

Well, after that fateful summer night dinner in Maine, never again, shall Nancy and I not take the opportunity to step-up-to-the-plate and defend the principles of diversity, tolerance and equality.

Nancy and I encourage you to take the same pledge.

Certainly, there are plenty of opportunities these days to practice what we preach.

As I write these words, the 2012 United States Presidential Election is in full swing.

It has been said, and I'm sure you have heard, that "all is fair in love, war, and politics." Sadly, some among us, especially demagogues, are all-too-willing to take advantage of and to appeal directly to peoples' primary emotions of fear, anger, and disgust in attempting to manipulate opinions and win votes.

A generally accepted definition of 'demagogue' may be found online as follows:

> A demagogue … or rabble-rouser is a political leader who appeals to the emotions, prejudices, and ignorance of the poorer and less educated classes in order to gain power. Demagogues usually oppose deliberation and advocate immediate, violent action to address a national crisis; they accuse moderate and thoughtful opponents of weakness. Demagogues have appeared in democracies since 410 B.C. Athens. They exploit a fundamental weakness in democracy: because ultimate power is held by the people, nothing stops the people from giving that power to someone

who appeals to the lowest common denominator of
a large segment of the population. Available online
at: http://en.wikipedia.org/wiki/Demagogue.

The 44th United States President, Barack Hussein Obama, who was elected to a first term in 2008, is our country's first bi-racial president.

Born on August 4, 1961, in Hawaii, his mother, Stanley Ann Dunham, had been born in Wichita, Kansas, and was of mostly English ancestry, along with Scottish, Irish, German, and Swiss. His father, Barack Obama, Sr., was a black man from the African country of Kenya.

From the moment he became a serious contender to become the nominee of the Democratic party in 2007, he became a target of hate on the part of those racists and bigots among us who could not fathom, let alone accept, the idea of an African-American as being worthy of the presidency.

His early haters chose to define him as inferior and unworthy because of the color of his skin only, basing their irrational conclusions on unsubstantiated and false stereotypes, and totally ignoring Obama's exceptional qualities as a human being and as an accomplished professional.

His haters totally ignored or were oblivious to the facts that Obama actually reflected and represented the ideal, self-made American man. He was honest, hard-working, and dedicated to his family, country, and his profession. He was and continues to be, in fact, the complete and noble embodiment of someone who has realized The American Dream.

Barack Obama is a graduate of Columbia University and Harvard Law School, where he was president of the prestigious *Harvard Law Review*.

Before earning his law degree, he was a community organizer in Chicago, where he worked with local churches organizing job training and other programs for poor and working-class residents of Altgeld Gardens, a public housing project, "where 5,300 African-Americans tried to survive amid shuttered steel mills, a nearby landfill, a putrid sewage treatment plant, and a pervasive feeling that the white establishment of Chicago would never give them a fair shake."

Obama's haters also ignored or discounted the realities that he also worked as a civil rights attorney in Chicago and taught constitutional law at the University of Chicago Law School from 1992 to 2004.

He also served three terms representing the 13th District in the Illinois Senate from 1997 to 2004.

Haters love to ignore these inconvenient truths, relying instead on their racist and bigoted values and beliefs, rooted in their primitive emotions of fear, anger, and disgust, and bolstered by their smug and self-satisfied ignorance.

As I mentioned above, the 2012 presidential campaign is well underway, as I write the final chapter of this book.

Throughout the Republican presidential primaries of earlier this year, we observed certain Republican presidential contenders and their supporters repeatedly engaging in demagoguery by attempting to characterize Obama as being the "Other," someone who is not like us, someone who is different, foreign, exotic, suspicious, untrustworthy, unreliable, and, certainly, not fit to be president.

They did this by not-so-subtle appeals to racist values and beliefs, and those appeals have continued, unabated, throughout the campaign season. Sadly, their messages have resonated among the haters, and they have probably colored the perceptions of non-haters as well.

Two prominent and recurring examples of this practice are the outrageous and demonstrably false claims of the "birthers," and the repeated references to Obama as "the food-stamp president."

Among the "birthers," are the billionaire Donald Trump, the right-wing hate-mongering talk radio host, Rush Limbaugh, and, last but not least, Republican presidential nominee, Mitt Romney, along with many of his stalwart supporters, including several elected U.S. congresspersons, senators, and state governors and legislators.

At base, are the racist beliefs of numerous birthers in the Tea Party and fellow-travelers, whose votes are seen as essential to ensuring the success of the Republican Party in the November, 2012, presidential election.

Despite the ready and easy public availability of Obama's Hawaiian birth certificate, no amount of hard, verifiable evidence will convince this crowd of bigots and ignoramuses that a black guy with a name like Barack Hussein Obama is actually a citizen of the United States.

He looks foreign, his name sounds foreign, so he must, *ipso facto* and duh, be foreign.

Equally pernicious, despicable, and inexcusable is the frequent reference to our nation's duly elected, native-born, leader as the "food-stamp president," a shameful attempt to appeal to racist stereotypes of African-Americans as "lazy, shiftless Niggers," as they were once so cavalierly, and often still are, in not-so-polite circles, referred to by their white haters.

These same ignorers of fact and truth are apparently totally oblivious to the reality that the vast majority of welfare recipients in the United States are actually white people. Furthermore, most healthy, able-bodied people, regardless of their skin color, would actually rather be working at a full-time job than being on welfare.

Surely, we're better than this, and we have a moral responsibility, both as U.S. citizens, and as human beings, to confront the president's birther and food-stamp detractors, whenever they rear their ugly, disgusting, and hateful heads.

Don't be shy. Call it like it is. It is hateful, despicable, and way, way, way beneath human dignity!

In this regard, it is important to recognize the obvious, if disappointing and depressing, linkages between the images invoked by the birthers and "food-stamp president" advocates and the stories we discussed in Chapter 3.

Specifically, it is difficult to miss the connections between the birther and food stamp rhetoric and the "Stranger (vs. in-group) (-I, C), Impure other (vs. pure in-group) (-I), and Animal pest (vs. human) (-I, P) stories, as those stories were described by former President of the American Psychological Association, Robert J. Sternberg, and Karin Sternberg (2008, pp. 84-95).

In addition to what each of us can do, personally, to demonstrate our respect for diversity, teach tolerance, and fight hate, we can join with other like-minded defenders of freedom and equality in organized efforts to combat our common enemies.

Joining Others in Efforts to Respect Diversity, Teach Tolerance, and Fight Hate

In most local communities, counties, and states, throughout our great nation, you can find informal and formal groups and organizations whose missions, agendas, and activities reveal their commitments to respect for diversity, teaching tolerance and fighting manifest hate.

Most, although not all, of these are recognizable as progressive organizations; namely, those that work to change those aspects of the *status quo* that resist or reject diversity and tolerance.

Progressives are most likely to self-identify as liberals and members of the Democratic Party, although progressives can be found among Independents and Republicans as well.

It was the progressive movements in our history that fought for and gained greater equality for women and members of minority groups, despite serious and often violent opposition from those vested in the *status quo*, especially wealthy, and even non-so-wealthy, white men.

In my first language, French, there is an old adage that reads, "*Plus ça change, plus c'est la même chose*," which means simply that "The more things change, the more they stay the same."

This truism, sadly but truly, applies to intolerance and hate, in all their evil and despicable motivations and manifestations.

Because of this reality, it is vitally important that you, not only live exemplary lives of love and tolerance, and combat manifest hate at every opportunity, but that you also seek out and join with like-minded others in unified and organized efforts to stop hate dead in its ugly, stinkin' tracks.

If you make the effort to seek them out, such groups are not hard to find. Nancy, my wife, and I, for example, are members of the Piedmont Humanists in Upstate South Carolina.

These folks, who actually differ among themselves regarding their positions on various economic, political, and social issues, share the common values, beliefs, and commitments to respect for diversity and tolerance, including tolerances of differences pertaining to religious beliefs and practices, and also incorporating and supporting the right of unbelief, free-thought, agnosticism, and atheism.

Above all, they are open-minded, ever-ready to consider new facts and reasonable arguments, even if they run counter to previously held beliefs and positions on the issues. If they are intolerant of anything, it is racism, misogyny, and intolerance, itself. And, they are not afraid to act upon their beliefs when necessary.

Nancy and I are comfortable in their presence.

Such groups, in their many varieties, are, no doubt, represented in your own community. In that regard, don't overlook progressive church groups and civic organizations, such as the A.C.L.U., or the American Civil Liberties Union, of which I am a proud card-carrying member and supporter.

It is curious that the A.C.L.U. is a frequent target of the fanatic right, since its primary mission is to defend the *United States Constitution*, and especially the Constitution's amendments.

What could possibly motivate anyone to object to an organization dedicated to protecting freedom of speech, freedom of religion, freedom of the press, the right to assemble peacefully and protest the government, women's rights, the rights of minorities, and so on, *unless* their goal was to deny those very same rights to those "Others" who were different from them.

Please allow me to indulge my freedom of speech when I respond to this nonsense as being utterly and undeniably best characterized by the acronym 'PPP,' pathetic, perverse, and putrid.

Beyond joining and otherwise supporting local, county, and state diversity-tolerance-and-manifest hate-fighting groups and organizations, do what you can to support the efforts of such groups and organizations that operate at the national level.

Supporting National Organizations that are Dedicated to Promoting Respect for Diversity, Teaching Tolerance, and Fighting Manifest Hate

Earlier in the book, I singled out, for special mention, three such organizations; namely, the Anti-Defamation League (ADL), the Political Research Associates (PRA), and the Southern Poverty Law Center

(SPLC), and I briefly described, especially in Chapter 4, their stated missions and areas of activity.

Any and all of these organizations are worthy of your involvement and support.

Just visit their websites at www.adl.org, www.publiceye.org, and www.splcenter.org to learn more about their noble missions and how you can, personally, become involved and supportive.

It's the right and necessary thing to do. You can do it. I know that you can, and have full confidence that you will!

Fighting those Stressors in our Social Environments that are Likely to Trigger the Feelings of Existential Insecurity that are so Closely Related to Hate

In Chapter 5, where I presented the results of my own research on manifest hate, I pointed out that there has been a growing body of well-documented social-scientific research demonstrating relationships between existential insecurity and a wide variety of social problems.

In that regard, I mentioned the contributions by Peter Corning in his *The Fair Society*; by Richard Wilkinson and Kate Pickett in their *The Spirit Level: Why Greater Equality Makes Societies Stronger*; and by Pippa Norris and Ronald Inglehart in their *Sacred and Secular: Religion and Politics World Wide*.

I then went on to present and discuss with you the results of my own research, showing that my findings were consistent with and supported those of these contemporary researchers.

I did this by formulating and testing 22 hypotheses regarding the relationships between manifest hate, as measured by my HATE RATE, and 22 measures or indicators of existential insecurity. In each and every instance, the associated statistical tests produced findings supporting or confirming the hypotheses.

Among the sources of existential insecurity singled out in the hypotheses were the economic stressors of income inequality, low levels of educational attainment, membership in a racial or ethnic minority, gender inequality, inequalities of health and mortality, crime and punishment, and extreme religiosity.

Since all of the above sources of existential insecurity relate to manifest hate, it would behoove us to work toward reducing high levels of inequality whenever we can.

Based upon my own previous and closely related research, I recommend that we focus our efforts first and foremost on reducing levels of economic inequality, both income and wealth inequality.

If you read my recent book, *Economic Inequality and What YOU Can Do About It: A Primer and Call to Action!*, you will recall that I found that the existential insecurity arising from the economic stressor of income inequality was found to be related to a wide variety of measures of societal dysfunction or social problems, including the violent crime rate, the teen pregnancy and birth rates, the overall health and well-being of state populations, the infant mortality rate, the life expectancy, the high school completion rate, and the percentages of blacks and females in state populations.

These very same relationships were found and reported in this book, but in this case the primary variable of interest was manifest hate, as measured by my HATE RATE, as opposed to existential insecurity, as measured by the Gini Coefficient of income inequality.

To fight income inequality, and most other forms of inequality, for that matter, is to fight also manifest hate.

In my book on economic inequality, I answered the question posed by my Chapter 9, title *"Question: What, if Anything, Can and Should YOU do About it"*, by responding *"Identify and Prioritize Key Issues; Stay Informed; and Get Involved!"*

Altogether I identified and prioritized 7 key issues. They were universal health care; access to affordable quality education from preschool and kindergarten through graduate and professional school; a living wage, as opposed to a minimum wage, for all workers; a maximum wage for occupations, especially corporate CEOs in the financial sector; government investment in infrastructure and research and development; more progressive taxation of both income and wealth, especially inherited wealth; and political reform.

This agenda for reducing economic inequality is also an agenda for reducing levels of manifest hate.

My book on economic inequality also discussed various ways you can stay informed and get involved. I encourage you to read or reread those sections and act upon some of the suggestions, to the extent that time allows.

Thank you for hearing me out, even with my feeble, hither and "yawn," attempts at humor, my new friend.

With all best wishes for success in our joint efforts to promote diversity, teach tolerance, and fight hate,

Richard G. Dumont, Ph.D.

Greenville, South Carolina

Please keep in touch by emailing me at: whenhatehappens@gmail.com.

APPENDIX PART I

STATE NAMES AND VARIABLES APPEARING IN FIGURES 1 THROUGH 22
OF CHAPTER 6.

IN FIGURES 1 THROUGH 4

STATE	IN ALL FIGURES HATERATE	IN FIGURE 1 GINI	IN FIGURE 2 MDINCOME	IN FIGURE 3 POVERTY	IN FIGURE 4 TTPTBTPR
AL	2.41	0.4717	40554	16.9	7.1
AK	0.235	0.4164	64333	8.9	5.8
AZ	0.895	0.4511	49889	14.2	7.7
AR	2.53	0.4578	38134	17.9	6.9
CA	0.645	0.4687	59948	12.4	7.6
CO	1.065	0.4494	55212	12	6.8
CT	0.515	0.4809	65967	7.9	6.9
DE	1.515	0.4317	54610	10.5	5.8
DC	4.735	0.5432	54317	16.4	12.4
FL	0.96	0.4679	47804	12.1	7.6
GA	1.31	0.4616	49136	14.3	6.4
HI	0.125	0.4274	63746	8	6.9
ID	1.735	0.4277	46253	12.1	5.6
IL	0.65	0.4634	54124	11.9	6.8
IN	0.855	0.4296	47448	12.3	6.4
IA	1.37	0.4232	47292	11	5.4
KS	0.82	0.4413	47451	11.2	6.5
KY	0.81	0.4607	40267	17.3	7.6
LA	1.875	0.4768	40926	18.6	7.6
ME	0.38	0.4353	45888	12	6.5
MD	0.755	0.4385	68080	8.3	7.2
MA	0.73	0.4643	62365	9.9	7.3
MI	0.805	0.4463	47950	14	6.7
MN	0.535	0.4316	55802	9.5	5.8
MS	2.65	0.4732	36338	20.6	7.1
MO	1.7	0.4485	45114	13	6
MT	3.075	0.4349	43531	14.1	5.9
NE	0.735	0.4278	47085	11.2	5.6
NV	1.77	0.4368	55062	10.7	5.9
NH	0.99	0.4151	62369	7.1	6
NJ	1.59	0.461	67035	8.6	7.5
NM	0.25	0.4591	41452	18.1	7.2
NY	0.465	0.4985	53514	13.7	8.1
NC	1.035	0.4612	44670	14.3	7.4
ND	0.515	0.4356	43753	12.1	5.6

OH	0.715	0.4454	46597	13.1	6.4
OK	1.54	0.4605	41567	15.9	6.3
OR	0.74	0.4464	48730	12.9	6.3
PA	0.785	0.4563	48576	11.6	7
RI	0.785	0.4502	53568	12	6.8
SC	2.99	0.4593	43329	15	7
SD	1.435	0.434	43424	13.1	5.3
TN	1.99	0.4675	42367	15.9	7.7
TX	0.895	0.4738	47548	16.3	8.1
UT	0.665	0.4104	55109	9.7	5.8
VT	0.815	0.4284	49907	10.1	6
VA	1.02	0.4547	59562	9.9	7.2
WA	0.68	0.4447	55591	11.4	7.2
WV	2.455	0.453	37060	16.9	7
WI	0.53	0.4247	50578	10.8	5.5
WY	1.855	0.4215	51731	8.7	5.2

APPENDIX PART II

STATE NAMES AND VARIABLES APPEARING IN FIGURES 1 THROUGH 22
OF CHAPTER 6.

IN FIGURES 5 THROUGH 9

IN ALL FIGURES STATE	IN FIGURE 5 HSORMORE	IN FIGURE 6 %BLACK	IN FIGURE 7 %HISGRTH	IN FIGURE 8 %FEMALE	IN FIGURE 9 OBESITY
AL	82.1	26.5	145	51.6	30.1
AK	92	4.1	52	47.9	27.3
AZ	83.1	4	46	49.9	23.3
AR	82.5	15.8	114	51	28.1
CA	80.8	6.7	28	50	23.1
CO	90	4.2	41	49.6	18.4
CT	88.4	10.3	50	51.2	20.8
DE	86	20.9	96	51.5	25.9
DC	83.3	55.2	22	52.7	22.1
FL	86.7	15.9	57	50.9	23.3
GA	84.2	30	96	50.8	27.5
HI	88.7	2.9	38	49.6	20.7
ID	88.9	0.9	73	49.7	24.6
IL	87.6	15	32	50.7	25.3
IN	88.2	9	82	50.7	27.5
IA	90.4	2.6	84	50.6	26.3
KS	90.2	6.1	59	50.3	25.8
KY	79.9	7.7	122	51.1	28.4
LA	79.7	31.9	79	51.5	29.5
ME	89.3	1	81	51.2	23.7
MD	87.2	29.5	106	51.6	25.2
MA	89.9	6.9	46	51.5	20.9
MI	89.7	14.3	35	50.8	27.7
MN	93	4.5	75	50.2	24.8
MS	81.1	37.2	106	51.5	31.7
MO	87.1	11.5	79	51.1	27.4
MT	91.4	0.6	58	49.9	21.7
NE	91	4.4	77	50.4	26.5
NV	85.6	8	82	49.1	23.6
NH	91.6	1.2	79	50.7	23.6
NJ	86.7	14.5	39	51	22.9
NM	81.8	2.9	25	50.7	23.3
NY	85.1	17.4	19	51.5	23.5
NC	84.2	21.7	111	51	27.1
ND	88.7	1	73	49.8	25.9

APPENDIX PART III

STATE NAMES AND VARIABLES APPEARING IN FIGURES 1 THROUGH 22
OF CHAPTER 6.

			IN FIGURES 10 THROUGH 14		
IN ALL	IN FIGURE	IN FIGURE	IN FIGURE	IN FIGURE	IN FIGURE
FIGURES	10	11	12	13	14
STATE	SMOKRATE	PREGRATE	BIRTHS	HEALTH	WELLBEIN
AR	22.5	93	66	-8.1	62.8
CA	22.2	96	47	5.3	66.5
CO	19.8	82	51	9.7	67.3
CT	22.4	70	31	17.5	66.3
DE	14.3	93	48	-1.6	64.7
DC	18.7	128	56	N.A.	N.A.
FL	15.5	97	51	-8.9	64.8
GA	19	95	63	-7.8	66.1
HI	17.3	93	46	21.6	70.2
ID	19.3	62	43	16.1	67.1
IL	19.3	87	48	0.8	65.8
IN	17	73	49	-0.6	63.9
IA	19.2	55	35	11.6	67.6
KS	20.2	69	46	6.7	67.2
KY	24.1	76	56	-3.6	62.3
LA	19.8	87	62	-15.2	64.2
ME	17.9	52	29	15.3	66.7
MD	28.3	91	41	3.4	66.8
MA	22.6	60	26	17.7	66.6
MI	20.1	75	40	2	64.9
MN	17.1	50	30	18.8	67.8
MS	16.4	103	71	-15	64
MO	21.2	74	49	-4.9	64.8
MT	16.5	60	37	6.5	68.3
NE	24	59	38	12	66.3
NV	24.6	113	61	-7.9	63.8
NH	19.5	47	23	19.9	66.9
NJ	19.9	90	32	9.8	65.6
NM	21.5	103	66	1.7	65.3
NY	19.4	91	33	3.8	65
NC	17.2	95	59	-3.2	65.1
ND	20.8	42	28	12.5	67.3
OH	18.9	74	46	0.7	63.6
OK	22.9	86	60	-8.1	64.2
OR	21	79	43	11.3	66
PA	23.1	60	34	2	65.4

RI	25.8	67	34	14	64.2
SC	16.9	89	59	-10.7	64.9
SD	20.9	54	38	7.5	66.5
TN	17	89	60	-9.7	64
TX	21.9	101	69	-9	66.2
UT	19.8	53	39	18.2	68.3
VT	24.3	44	24	24.8	67.4
VA	19.4	72	41	9	67
WA	11.7	75	39	14.9	66.8
WV	17.6	67	47	-5	60.5
WI	18.6	55	35	10.3	66
WY	16.8	77	42	11.8	66.7

APPENDIX PART IV

		IN FIGURES 15 THROUGH 19			
IN ALL FIGURES	IN FIGURE 15	IN FIGURE 16	IN FIGURE 17	IN FIGURE 18	IN FIGURE 19
STATE	INFANMOR	LIFEXEP	HDI	VICRATE	MURRATE
AL	7.9	74.4	4.09	425	8.3
AK	5.3	77.1	5.27	688	5.4
AZ	6.4	77.5	5.11	501	7.5
AR	5.8	75.2	3.87	552	7.3
CA	9	78.2	5.56	533	6.8
CO	14.1	78.2	5.65	392	3.3
CT	7.2	78.7	6.3	281	3.1
DE	8.2	76.8	5.33	682	4.9
DC	6.5	72	6.21	1508	29.1
FL	6.1	77.5	5.07	712	6.2
GA	7.4	75.3	4.86	471	6.4
HI	8	80	5.73	281	1.6
ID	5.3	77.9	4.65	247	2.5
IL	7.4	76.4	5.39	542	6.1
IN	6.6	76.1	4.74	315	5.8
IA	10.1	78.3	5.06	284	1.8
KS	6.9	77.3	5.06	425	4.6
KY	7.3	75.2	4.23	263	4
LA	5.2	74.2	4.07	698	12.4
ME	7.9	77.6	4.89	116	1.7
MD	5.1	76.3	5.96	679	9.7
MA	11.4	78.4	6.24	447	2.9
MI	7.5	76.3	4.99	562	7.1
MN	7	78.8	5.74	312	2.4
MS	5.6	73.6	3.93	299	7.7
MO	5.8	75.9	4.68	546	6.3
MT	5.3	77.2	4.49	254	1.8
NE	5.2	77.8	5.05	282	2.8
NV	6.1	75.8	4.78	742	9
NH	5.8	78.3	5.73	139	1
NJ	8.8	77.5	6.16	352	4.9
NM	6	77	4.56	643	6.8
NY	8.3	77.7	5.77	435	4.8
NC	8.1	75.8	4.64	476	6.1
ND	5.9	78.3	4.92	128	1.3
OH	7.3	76.2	4.87	350	4.7
OK	6.5	75.2	4.15	497	5.8
OR	9.4	77.8	5.03	280	2.3

PA	7.2	76.7	5.12	439	5.9
RI	8.9	78.3	5.56	228	2.6
SC	6.6	74.8	4.36	766	8.3
SD	4.5	77.7	4.82	171	1.2
TN	6.5	75.1	4.33	760	6.8
TX	7.5	76.7	4.67	516	5.9
UT	5.1	76.7	5.08	224	1.8
VT	8.1	78.2	5.27	137	1.9
VA	6.6	76.8	5.53	282	5.2
WA	6.8	78.2	5.53	346	3
WV	8.1	75.1	3.85	280	4.1
WI	6.6	77.9	5.23	284	3
WY	6.8	76.7	4.8	240	1.7

APPENDIX PART V

STATE NAMES AND VARIABLES APPEARING IN FIGURES 1 THROUGH 22 OF CHAPTER 6.

STATE	IN ALL FIGURES	IN FIGURE 20 INCARATE	IN FIGURE 21 HIGHREL	IN FIGURE 22 EVANPROT
AL		890	8.360133229	49
AK		705	-7.8299239	26
AZ		808	-2.91253301	23
AR		673	7.098260287	53
CA		682	-3.8464711	18
CO		728	-5.04645253	23
CT		544	-6.20014856	10
DE		820	-0.51036236	15
DC		553	-0.35723926	15
FL		835	-0.04045946	25
GA		1021	5.028804995	38
HI		447	-0.20486575	26
ID		784	1.001902226	22
IL		507	-1.22385134	19
IN		637	1.918898437	34
IA		412	-1.25235559	24
KS		582	2.866942554	25
KY		720	5.778185504	49
LA		1138	8.093229461	31
ME		273	-7.41326516	15
MD		636	-0.35723926	15
MA		356	-6.89062275	11
MI		663	-0.74530109	26
MN		300	-1.75435212	21
MS		955	11.87607746	47
MO		715	1.90148911	37
MT		526	-1.59411211	26
NE		421	1.277883108	21
NV		756	-2.85165595	13
NH		319	-8.66159046	11
NJ		532	-2.89446798	12
NM		782	-1.62970076	25
NY		482	-4.33262298	11
NC		620	5.823315259	41
ND		359	0.692860326	24
OH		559	-0.17497521	26

OK	919	5.148453356	53
OR	531	-4.28648346	30
PA	607	-0.52365865	18
RI	313	-6.20014856	10
SC	830	7.733582672	45
SD	622	0.692860326	24
TN	732	7.347121474	51
TX	976	4.297023797	34
UT	466	4.565205967	7
VT	317	-8.66159046	11
VA	759	1.027080716	31
WA	465	-3.21963495	25
WV	443	4.087713704	36
WI	653	-3.40682712	24
WY	690	-1.59411211	26

REFERENCES

Allport, Gordon W. 1954. *The Nature of Prejudice*. Cambridge, MA: Addison-Wesley.

Anti-Defamation League (ADL). 2008. *Anti-Defamation League*. Available online at: www.adl.org.

Bell, Jeannine. 2002. *Policing Hatred: Law Enforcement, Civil Rights, and Hate Crime*. New York: New York University Press.

Bennett, Susie, Nolan, James J., and Norman Conti. 2009. "Defining and Measuring Hate Crime: A Potpourri of Issues." In Perry, Barbara and Brian Levin (Eds.), *Hate Crimes: Vol. 1, Understanding and Defining Hate Crime* (pp. 163-182). Westport, CT: Praeger Publishers.

Berlet, Chip. 2004. "Mapping the Political Right: Gender and Race Oppression in Right-Wing Movements." In Ferber, Abby L. (Ed.), *Home Grown Hate: Gender and Organized Racism* (pp. 19-47). New York: Routledge.

Berrill, Kevin. 1992. "Anti-Gay Violence and Victimization in the United States: An Overview." In Herek, Gregory M. and Kevin Berrill (Eds.), *Hate Crimes: Confronting Violence Against Lesbians and Gay Men*. Newbury Park, CA: Sage Publications.

Best, Joel. 2007. *Social Problems*. New York: W. W. Norton & Company.

Bhatia, Rajani. 2004. "Green or Brown? White Nativist Environmental Movements." In Ferber, Abby L. (Ed.), *Home Grown Hate: Gender and Organized Racism* (pp. 205-225). New York: Routledge.

Blazak, Randy. 2004. "Getting it: The Role of Women in Male Desistance from Hate Groups." In Ferber, Abby L. (Ed.), *Home Grown Hate: Gender and Organized Racism* (pp. 161-179). New York: Routledge.

Blee, Kathleen M. 1991. *Women of the Klan: Racism and Gender in the 1920s.* Berkeley: University of California Press.

Blee, Kathleen M. 1996. "Becoming a Racist: Women in Contemporary Ku Klux Klan and Neo-Nazi Groups." *Gender and Society*, (10) 6: 680-702.

Blee, Kathleen M. 2002. *Inside Organized Racism: Women in the Hate Movement.* Berkeley: University of California Press.

Blee, Kathleen M. 2004. "Women and Organized Racism." In Ferber, Abby L. (Ed.), *Home Grown Hate: Gender and Organized Racism* (pp. 49-74). New York: Routledge.

Boeckmann, Robert J., Turpin-Petrosino, Carolyn, and Brian Levin. 2002. "Understanding the Harm of Hate Crime." *Journal of Social Issues*, (58) 2: 207-410.

Bullard, Sara. 1991. (Ed.) *The Ku Klux Klan: A History of Racism and Violence.* Montgomery, AL: Southern Poverty Law Center.

Buss, David M. 2005. *The Handbook of Evolutionary Psychology.* Hoboken, N.J.: John Wiley & Sons, Inc.

Chesler, Phyllis. 2003. *The New Anti-Semitism.* San Francisco, CA: Josey-Bass.

Corning, Peter. 2011. *The Fair Society: The Science of Human Nature and the Pursuit of Social Justice.* Chicago: The University of Chicago Press.

Damasio, Antonio. 2010. *The Feeling of What Happens: Body and Emotion in the Making of Consciousness.* New York: Mariner Books.

Daniels, Jessie. 2009. *Cyber Racism*. New York: Rowman and Littlefield.

Delamontagne, R. Georges. 2010. "High Religiosity and Societal Dysfunction in the United States during the First Decade of the Twenty-First Century." *Evolutionary Psychology*, 8(4): 617–657. Available online at: www.epjournal.net/filestore/EP08617657.pdf.

Delamontagne, R. Georges. 2012. "Relationships between Varieties of Religious Experience and Manifest Hate: A Sociological Analysis." *Journal of Religion and Society*, 14: 1-25. Available online at: http://moses.creighton.edu/JRS/2012/2012-23.pdf.

Dobratz, Betty A., and Shanks-Meile, Stephanie L. 1997. *"White Power, White Pride" The White Separatist Movement in the United States*. New York: Wayne Publishers.

Dobratz, Betty A., and Shanks-Meile, Stephanie L. 2004. "The White Separatist Movement: Worldviews on Gender, Feminism, Nature, and Change." In Ferber, Abby L. (Ed.), *Home Grown Hate: Gender and Organized Racism* (pp. 113-141). New York: Routledge.

Ehrilch, Howard. 2009. *Hate Crimes and Ethnoviolence*. Boulder, CO: Westview Press.

Ekman, Paul, Levenson, Robert W., and Wallace V. Friesen. 1983. "Autonomic Nervous System Activity Distinguishes between Emotions." *Science*, 221: 1208-1210.

Feagin, Joe R. 2000. *Racist America: Roots, Current Realities, and Future Reparations*. New York: Routledge.

Feagin, Joe R., Baker, David V., and Clairece Booher Feagin. 2005. *Social Problems: A Critical Power-Conflict Perspective*. Upper Saddle River, NJ: Prentice Hall.

Feagin, Joe R. and Hernán Vera. 1995. *White Racism*. New York: Routledge.

Federal Bureau of Investigation. 2009. *Hate Crime Statistics*. Available online at: http://www2.fbi.gov/ucr/hc2009/index.html.

Ferber, Abby L. 2004. (Ed.) *Home Grown Hate: Gender and Organized Racism*. New York: Routledge.

Ferber, Abby L. and Michael S. Kimmel. 2004. "White Men Are This Nation: Right-Wing Militias and the Restoration of Rural American Masculinity." In Ferber, Abby L. (Ed.), *Home Grown Hate: Gender and Organized Racism* (pp. 143-160). New York: Routledge.

Fox, James Alan and Jack Levin. 2006. *The Will to Kill: Explaining Senseless Murder*. Boston, MA: Allyn and Bacon.

Gallup-Healthways. 2008. *The Well-Being Index*. Available online at: www.well-beingindex.com.

Gerstenfeld, Phyllis B. 2004. *Hate Crimes: Causes, Controls, and Controversies*. Thousand Oaks, CA: Sage.

Goodheart, Annette. 1994. *Laughter Therapy: How to Laugh about Everything in Your Life That Isn't Really Funny*. Santa Barbara: Less Stress Press.

Grattet, Ryken and Valerie Jenness. 2001. The Birth and Maturation of Hate Crime Policy in the United States." *American Behavioral Scientist*, 45: 668-696.

Guttmacher Institute. 2010. "U.S. Teenage Pregnancies, Births and Abortions: National and State Trends and Trends by Race and Ethnicity." Available online at: www.guttmacher.org/pubs/FB-ATSRH.html.

Guttmacher Institute. 2010. "Ranking by Rates of Pregnancy, Birth and Abortion and the Rates Themselves among Women Aged 15-19, by Age Group, According to State of Residence, 2000." Available online at: www.guttmacher.org/pubs/USTPtrends.pdf.

Hamm, Mark S. 1994). *Hate Crime: International Perspectives on Causes and Control*. Cincinnati, OH: Anderson.

Harvard Institute for Global Health and the Harvard School of PublicHealth. 2006. "Top States for Life Expectancy." Available online at: www.webmd.com/news/20060913/top-states-for-life-expectancy?page=2.

Heiner, Robert. 2010. *Conflicting Interests: Readings in Social Problems and Inequality*. New York: Oxford University Press.

Heiner, Robert. 2010. *Social Problems: An Introduction to Critical Constructionism*. New York: Oxford University Press.

Holthouse, David. 2009. "The Year in Hate." *Intelligence Report*, 133: 48-69.

Iganski, Paul. 2008. *Hate Crime and The City*. Bristol, U.K.: The Policy Press.

Immigration Works USA. 2010. "To Copy or Not to Copy?" Available online at: www.immigrationworksusa.org/uploaded/IW_AZ_copycats_report.pdf.

Jacobs, James B. and Kimberly Potter. 1997. "Hate Crimes: A Critical Perspective." In Tonry, Michael (Ed.), *Crime and Justice: A Review of Research*. Chicago, IL: University of Chicago Press.

Jacobs, James B. and Kimberly Potter. 1998. *Hate Crimes: Criminal Law and Identity Politics*. New York: Oxford University Press.

Jenness, Valerie. 2004. "The Dilemma of Difference: Gender and Hate Crime Policy." In Ferber, Abby L. (Ed.), *Home Grown Hate: Gender and Organized Racism* (pp. 181-203). New York: Routledge.

Jenness, Valerie. Kendal Broad. 1997. *Hate Crimes: New Social Movements and the Politics of Violence*. New York: Aldine De Gruyter.

Jenness, Valerie and Ryken Grattet. 2004. *Making Hate a Crime: From Social Movement to Law Enforcement.* New York: Russell Sage Foundation.

Kemper, Theodore D. 1987. "How Many Emotions are There? Wedding the Social and Autonomic Components." *The American Journal of Sociology,* 93(2): 263-289.

Lawrence, Frederick M. 1999. *Punishing Hate: Bias Crimes under American Law.* Cambridge, MA: Harvard University Press.

Levin, Jack. and Jack McDevitt. 1993. *Hate Crimes: The Rising Tide of Bigotry and Bloodshed.* New York: Plenum.

Levin, Jack and Jack McDevitt. 1995. "The Research Needed to Understand Hate Crime." *Chronicle of Higher Education,* 41(47): B1-2.

Levin, Jack and Jack McDevitt. 1995. "Landmark Study Reveals Hate Crimes Vary Significantly by Offender Motivation." *Klanwatch Intelligence Report,* 79.

Levin, Jack and Jack McDevitt. 2002. *Hate Crimes Revisited: America's War Against Those Who are Different.* Boulder, CO: Westview Press.

Levin, Jack and Jim Nolan. 2011. *The Violence of Hate: Confronting Racism, Anti-Semitism, and Other Forms of Bigotry.* Boston, MA: Allyn and Bacon.

Levin, Jack and Gordana Rabrenovic. 2001. "Hate Crimes and Ethnic Conflict: An Introduction." *American Behavioral Scientist,* 45(4): 574-588.

Levin, Jack and Gordana Rabrenovic. 2004. *Why we Hate.* Amherst, N.Y.: Prometheus Books.

Levin, Jack and Gordana Rabrenovic. 2009. "Hate as Cultural Justification for Violence." In Levin, Brian (Ed.), *Understanding and Defining Hate Crime* (pp. 41-54). Westport, CT: Praeger.

Lieberman, Michael, and Steven M. Freeman. 2009. "Confronting Violent Bigotry: Hate Crime Laws and Legislation." In Perry, Barbara and Frederick Lawrence. (Eds.), *Hate Crimes: Vol. 5, Responding to Hate Crime* (pp. 1-30). Westport, CT: Praeger.

McIntosh, Peggy. 2004. "Afterword: The Growing Influence of Right-Wing Thought." In Ferber, Abby L. (Ed.), *Home Grown Hate: Gender and Organized Racism* (pp. 227-234). New York: Routledge.

McVeigh, Rory. 2004. "Structured Ignorance and Organized Racism in the United States." *Social Forces*, 82 (3): 895-936.

Murray, Charles. 2012. *Coming Apart: The State of White America 1960-2010.* New York: Cox and Murray, Inc.

Norris, Pippa and Ronald Inglehart. 2004. *Sacred and Secular: Religion and Politics Worldwide.* Cambridge , NY: Cambridge University Press.

Open Stat. 2009. Available online at: www.openstat.org. See also: www.statpages.org/miller/openstat/, the online version of William G. Miller's *Statistics and Measurement using Open Stat.*

Perry, Barbara. 2001. *In the Name of Hate: Understanding Hate Crimes.* New York: Routledge.

Perry, Barbara. 2004. "White Genocide: White Supremacists and the Politics of Reproduction." In Ferber, Abby L. (Ed.), *Home Grown Hate: Gender and Organized Racism* (pp. 75-95). New York: Routledge.

Pew Forum on Religion and Public Life. 2009. *U.S. Religious Landscape Survey.* Available online at: http://religions.pewforum.org/reports and at: http://religions.pewforum.org/maps.

Political Research Associates (PRA). 2011. "Researching the Right for Progressive Changemakers." Available online at: www.publiceye.org.

Potok, Mark. 2010. "Rage on the Right: The Year in Hate." *Intelligence Report* 137: 41-63.

Rogers, JoAnn and Jacquelyn S. Litt. 2004. "Normalizing Racism: A Case Study of Motherhood in White Supremacy." In Ferber, Abby L. (Ed.), *Home Grown Hate: Gender and Organized Racism* (pp. 97-112). New York: Routledge.

Rozin, Paul, Lowery, Laura, Imada, Sumino, and Jonathan Haidt. 1999. "The CAD Triad Hypothesis: A Mapping between Three Moral Emotions (Contempt, Anger, Disgust) and Three Moral Codes (Community, Autonomy, Divinity)." *Journal of Personality and Social Psychology*, 76(4): 574-586.

Sherif, Muzafer. 1988. *The Robbers Cave Experiment: Intergroup Conflict and Cooperation*. Indianapolis, IN: Wesleyan.

Shweder, Richard A, Much, Nancy C, Mahapatra, Manomahan, and Lawrence Park. 1997. "The Big Three' of Morality (Autonomy, Community, Divinity) and the 'Big Three' Explanations of Suffering." In Brandt, Arnold and Paul Rozin (Eds.), *Morality and Health* (pp. 119-169). New York: Routledge.

Social Science Research Council. 2010. "The Modified American Development Index." Available online at: www.measureofamerica.org/human-development/.

Southern Poverty Law Center (SPLC). 1998. *Intelligence Report*, 89. Available online at: www.splcenter.org.

Southern Poverty Law Center (SPLC). 2010. *Intelligence Report*, 137. Available online at: www.splcenter.org.

Sternberg, Robert J. 1986. "A Triangular Theory of Love." *Psychological Review*, 93: 119-135.

Sternberg, Robert J. 1988. *The Triangle of Love*. New York: Basic Books.

Sternberg, Robert J. 1994. "Love is a Story." *The General Psychologist*, 30 (1): 1-11.

Sternberg, Robert J. 1997. "Construct Validation of a Triangular Love Scale." *European Journal of Social Psychology*, 27(3): 313-335.

Sternberg, Robert J. 1998. *Cupid's Arrow: The Course of Love through Time*. New York: Cambridge University Press.

Sternberg, Robert J. 2003. "A Duplex Theory of Hate: Development and Application to Terrorism, Massacres, and Genocide." *Review of General Psychology*, 7 (3): 299-328.

Sternberg, Robert L. 2005. (Ed.). *The Psychology of Hate*. Washington, D.C.: American Psychological Association.

Sternberg, Robert J. 2006. "A Duplex Theory of Love." In Sternberg, Robert J. and Karin Weis, (Eds.), *The New Psychology of Love* (pp. 184-199). New Haven, CT: Yale University Press.

Sternberg, R.J., and Karin Sternberg. 2008. *The Nature of Hate*. New York: Cambridge University Press.

Tooby, John and Leda Cosmides. 2005. "Conceptual Foundations of Evolutionary Psychology." In Buss, David M. (Ed.), *The Handbook of Evolutionary Psychology* (pp. 5-67). Hoboken, N.J.: John Wiley & Sons, Inc.

Trust for American's Health. 2009. "Obesity Rates, % Adults (2004-07 BMI Average." Available online at: http://healthyamericans.org/states/states.php?measure=obesity&sort=state.

United Health Foundation. 2009. "2009 Overall Rankings ... by State." Available online at: www.americashealthrankings.org.

U.S. Bureau of Justice Statistics. 2005. "Prison and Jail Inmates at Midyear 2005." Available online at: www.ojp.usdoj.gov/bjs/pub/pdf/pjim05.pdf.

U.S. Census Bureau. 2005. "State Rankings – Statistical Abstract of the United States: Infant Mortality Rate – 2005." Available online at: www.census.gov/compendia/ranks/rank17.html.

U.S. Census Bureau. 2008. "Small Area Income and Poverty Estimates in the United States: 2007." Available online at: http://manyeyes.alphaworks.ibm.com/manyeyes/visualizations/us-gini-coefficient-by-state-2006; http://enwikipedia.org/wiki/Houshold_income_in_the_United_States; and www.census.gov/compendia/statab/ranks/rank29.html.

U.S. Census Bureau. 2009. "Educational Attainment by State: 1990 to 2006." Available online at: www.census.gov/population/www/socdemo/educ-attn.html.

U.S. Census Bureau. 2010. "Percent of Total Population by Race and State." *The 2010 Statistical Abstract of the United States.* Available online at: http://www.census.gov/compendia/statab/cats/population.html.

U.S. Department of Justice, Federal Bureau of Investigation. 2006. "Crime Rates by State, 2005 and 2006, and by Type, 2006." Available online at: http://www.fbi.gov/ucr/clus2006/index.html/; also at http://en.wikipedia.org/wiki/List_of_countries_by_intentional_homicide_rate.

Weis, Karin. 2006. *Explorations of the Duplex Theory of Hate.* Berlin: Logos Verlag.

Weiss, Joan C. 1993. "Ethnoviolence's Impact upon and Response of Victims and the Community." In Kelly, R. (Ed.), *Bias Crime* (pp. 174-185). Chicago, IL: Office of International Criminal Justice.

Wilkinson, Richard and Kate Pickett. 2009. *The Spirit Level: Why Greater Equality Makes Societies Stronger.* New York: Bloomsbury Press.

About the Author:
Richard G. Dumont

Richard G. Dumont, a Maine native, earned his Ph.D. degree in Sociology at the University of Massachusetts at Amherst in 1968.

His previous publications include Economic Inequality and What YOU Can Do About It: A Primer And Call to Action!, as well as several articles and book reviews appearing in journals, such as the American Journal of Sociology, American Sociological Review, Sociology and Social Research, Journal of Higher Education, Research in Higher Education, Planning for Higher Education, Evoluntionary Psychology, Free Inquiry, and the Journal of Religion and Society. In the latter three, authorship was attributed to his French pseudonym, R. Georges Delamontagne.

He is currently retired from a thirty-plus year career in higher education teaching, research, and administration. His last two positions were those of President of the University of Maine at Fort Kent and University of Maine System Professor.

In 1994 he was awarded an Honorary Doctorate in Acadian Studies by the University of Moncton in New Brunswick, Canada. This was the first honorary doctorate granted by the university to a U.S. citizen, all previous honorees having been either Canadian or European.

He lives contentedly with his precious wife, Nancy, in beautiful Greenville, South Carolina.